MAYILAMMA

Jothibai Pariyadath, the transcriber of *Mayilamma: Oru Jeevitham*, is an acclaimed Malayalam poet, writer and translator. She published her first poetry collection, *Pesamadantha*, in 2009, and has translated the poems of Vladimir Mayakovsky into Malayalam as *Mayakovskyude Kavithakal* (2012). She received the Coimbatore Kerala Cultural Centre's literary prize for 2012. Her blog, *Kavyam Sugeyam*, featuring her recitations of more than five hundred Malayalam poems, is hugely popular.

Swarnalatha Rangarajan is Professor, Department of Humanities and Social Sciences, Indian Institute of Technology Madras, Chennai.

Sreejith Varma is Assistant Professor, Department of English, Christ Deemed-to-be University, Bengaluru, Karnataka.

MAYILAMMA

The Life of a Tribal Eco-Warrior

Jothibai Pariyadath

Translated from the original Malayalam by

SWARNALATHA RANGARAJAN

and

SREEJITH VARMA

With a Foreword by

SCOTT SLOVIC

Orient BlackSwan

MAYILAMMA: THE LIFE OF A TRIBAL ECO-WARRIOR

ORIENT BLACKSWAN PRIVATE LIMITED

Registered Office
3-6-752 Himayatnagar, Hyderabad 500 029, Telangana, India
e-mail: centraloffice@orientblackswan.com

Other Offices
Bengaluru, Bhopal, Chennai, Guwahati, Hyderabad,
Jaipur, Kolkata, Lucknow, Mumbai, New Delhi, Noida,
Patna, Vijayawada

First published 2018

ISBN 978-93-5287-359-3

Typeset in
Book Antiqua 10.5/12.6
by Le Studio Graphique, Gurgaon 122 001

027971

Printed in India at
Glorious Printers, Delhi

Published by
Orient Blackswan Private Limited
3-6-752, Himayatnagar, Hyderabad 500 029
e-mail: info@orientblackswan.com

Dedicated to
Mayilamma
and
her tribe of eco-warriors

CONTENTS

IMAGES

ACKNOWLEDGEMENTS

Translating Mayilamma's life story has been a long and rewarding journey and we would like to express our gratitude to the many people who saw us through this book—to all those who provided support, discussed things over and offered comments.

We are grateful to The Association for Studies in Literature and the Environment (ASLE-USA), a forum for studies in environmental humanities, for supporting us with the ASLE Translation Grant (2015) which helped us take the Mayilamma translation project forward in ever so many ways.

We would like to thank Prof. Scott Slovic (University of Idaho), one of the pioneering thinkers in the domain of environmental humanities, for the Foreword and his enthusiasm regarding this project.

We were encouraged by Dr Madhavi Menon and Ms Vidya Rao at Orient BlackSwan who nurtured this project from its early days. We owe our special thanks to them. We are also deeply appreciative of Ms Roopa Sharma at Orient BlackSwan for her warmth, ready help and most importantly for expediting the editing process. Our thanks are also due to Mr Suranjan Roy for his able copy editing and also for his great enthusiasm regarding Mayilamma's life work. This work was facilitated by Ms Jothibai Pariyadath, the collaborative transcriber-author of the Malayalam original, who showed a deep and abiding interest in this translation. We are deeply thankful to Mayilamma's family for their encouragement and support. Our sincere thanks are also due to Mr Vilayodi Venugopal, Chairman of the Anti-Coca-Cola Agitation Committee in Plachimada, and Mr Mariyappan, the President of the Adivasi Samrakshana Sangham, for their co-operation and support during interviews conducted by us.

We are indebted to the *Mathrubhumi* archives for giving us permission to use their evocative photographs. Special thanks are due to Mr Vinod and Mr Suresh for facilitating the process.

We would also like to thank Mr Madhuraj, Chief News Photographer in *Mathrubhumi* Periodicals, for giving us the permission to use photographs of the Plachimada struggle from his personal collection.

Our sincere thanks go out to the Department of Humanities and Social Sciences, IIT Madras, for providing us the space and time to work on this translation; Prof. R. Azhagarasan and Ms Uma Rangarajan for helping us with the nuances involved in decoding the folksongs of this narrative; to Nidheesh and Justin for helping us identify the exotically named fishes in this narrative; and to Prof. K. Srilata, Prof. Jyotirmaya Tripathy and Prof. Umakant Dash for their cordial support.

Swarnalatha Rangarajan
Sreejith Varma

FOREWORD

In September 2006, I sat with Vandana Shiva beneath a poster reading "This is Coke Pepsi Free Zone" in a small café in New Delhi, discussing how multinational companies employ data to achieve "the anesthesia of destruction", essentially numbing the public with numbers and technical information in order to stifle awareness and protest. At the time, I was unaware of the Plachimada Movement and similar struggles in India and elsewhere in the world, where local communities were responding to social and ecological crises caused by corporate exploitation of water resources in pursuit of profit. I asked Vandana to explain the sign on the wall above us, and she told me about the desperation of farmers in India who had lost the ability to maintain their traditional lifeways because of resource contamination and privatisation.

When I returned to the United States after that 2006 visit to India, I brought with me various pamphlets about the anti-Coke protests and various other social movements in South Asia, including efforts to resist the use of trademarked, genetically modified seeds, which made peasant farmers beholden to multinational behemoths such as Monsanto. I read these pamphlets and found many other journalistic and scientific reports about the ecological and social problems caused by multinationals in the developing world, and then I wrote a chapter called "Even Better than the Real Thing" for my 2008 book, *Going Away to Think: Engagement, Retreat, and Ecocritical Responsibility,* documenting my one-sided correspondence with the Coca-Cola Corporation, during which I repeatedly expressed my concerns about the company's activities in India and elsewhere by paper mail and email, each time receiving semi-anonymous replies from corporate PR staff members (only first names were used by respondents) in which the representatives assured me that Coca-Cola was a socially responsible company and was doing a sufficient job of monitoring its own activities in the developing world. Unsatisfied with the PR staff's efforts to quell my concerns, I wrote in my book about the company's negative impact on rural communities in India and about my frustrating efforts to communicate with corporate executives, and have continued to urge audiences to think twice about consuming Coca-Cola products when lecturing to high school and university students and teachers in Argentina, China, Poland, the United States, and various other countries around the world. Often my young listeners, who consume carbonated sugar water without appreciating the social consequences of irresponsible corporate behaviour, respond to my talks by saying they plan to change their soft drink consumption habits and stay away from Coke and Pepsi and even from bottled water (which is often sold by the same companies).

My personal efforts to intervene in the destructive practices of Coca-Cola are the small actions of an individual who happens to be privileged enough to have certain skills as a writer and public speaker and to have visited India and met with one of the leading activists concerned with the rights of rural communities. I understand it as my responsibility to use my education and my experiences to speak out about social injustice and environmental degradation, not simply to stick to narrow academic topics and circulate information among students and fellow scholars in the 'ivory tower'.

I was inspired to stop drinking Coca-Cola and to communicate about the corporate offences of the Coca-Cola Corporation as a result of reading activist pamphlets and scientific reports, but I did not have access to the powerful first-person narrative you now hold before you, *Mayilamma: The Life of a Tribal Eco-Warrior*, which was published in the Malayalam language in 2006 and is now appearing for the first time in English. I am grateful to Mayilamma herself for putting her struggles and her passion for social justice into words, to Jothibai Pariyadath for transcribing this story, and to Swarnalatha Rangarajan and Sreejith Varma for translating the work into a language that will now reach readers in many countries, and for contextualising the personal narrative in a powerful introduction. Words have power, and words that emerge from the authority of personal experience resonate with special force. *Mayilamma* is precisely this kind of story.

As the translators explain in their introduction, *Mayilamma* exemplifies a much larger genre of environmental justice narrative that encompasses not only several important Indian texts but works from as far away as Kenya and the United States. One could probably add Ken Saro-Wiwa's Nigerian memoir and Rigoberta Menchú's Guatemalan autobiography to the list, among others. It does not matter that Mayilamma herself was unable to read or write or that she was a tribal woman—rather, these aspects of her life contribute to the profound authenticity of her story and make it all the more admirable that she became such a strong activist in the face of multinational power and misdeeds. The Plachimada Movement is truly a David-and-Goliath Story, as Swarnalatha Rangarajan and Sreejith Varma say, but it is also a story that reinforces a fundamental faith in language and a refusal to quietly obey the world's destructive forces, whether corporate or governmental.

In her 1991 classic of American environmental literature, Terry Tempest Williams famously wrote, "The price of obedience has become too high," and told the story of a group of women who gathered at the Nevada Nuclear Test Site to protest the nuclear experiments performed by the American military. A few years later, Williams wrote the introduction to John Bradley's anthology *Atomic Ghost: Poets Respond to the Nuclear Age,* calling her essay "Throwing Flowers at Evil". Mayilamma's story is clear evidence of how an ordinary citizen with a fearless heart and a sense of right and wrong should respond when obedience becomes too costly and the only available weapon is story. Sometimes the world's destructive forces begin to wither when confronted with gentle truths expressed through flowers, poetry, or personal stories.

January 2018

Scott Slovic
Sunriver, Oregon, USA

A NOTE ON THE TRANSLATION

Mayilamma's life narrative stands testimony to the fact that the subalterns can indeed speak and that when they do so, they come into possession of an 'angelic strength' that can defeat behemoths and giants.

The Malayalam original, *Mayilamma: Oru Jeevitham* (2006), is a translator's challenge since it hybridises the autobiographical form by adopting the traditional oral mode of narration, which is central to the construction of the collective memory of tribal communities. Moreover, the narrative also employs a Malayalam-Tamil bricolage that is typical of borderlands between the states of Tamil Nadu and Kerala. Therefore a translation team of two turned out to be a huge advantage since both of us brought our individual strengths to this project. I, the first translator, am a native Tamil speaker who grew up in Kerala and studied Malayalam as a second language, and the second translator, Sreejith Varma, is a native Malayalam speaker who hails from Palakkad, which is close to Mayilamma's place. Varma's field visits to Plachimada and the interviews that he conducted with the local people and other important faces of the Plachimada struggle also play an important role in emplacing and contextualising Mayilamma's life-story.

We initially came up with our individual translations and while working together discovered that the translation opened up many spaces for interrogation, exchange and resonance. During the course of the translation work, we realised that proficiency in the three languages, viz. Malayalam, Tamil and English, was simply not enough. The final draft demanded a different order of discipline; we had to work intuitively and bring to the table knowledge from diverse sources.

Mayilamma and most of the Plachimada inhabitants identify themselves as Eravallars. According to Eravalla language experts, almost seventy per cent of the basic vocabulary forms in the language are similar to that of the Tamil vocabulary. This is true of Mayilamma's narrative in which the folk songs are rendered almost entirely in Tamil.

We are thankful to Jothibai Pariyadath's lucid, collaborative prose that has captured Mayilamma's oral rhythms with fidelity and has also lent structural continuity to a narrative that shuttles back and forth between the personal details of Mayilamma's life and the public dimensions of her participation and leadership in the Plachimada struggle. We have tried to keep the simplicity of the syntax intact in the translation. We are also thankful to Sugumaran's Tamil translation, *Mayilamma: Porattame Vazhkai* (2006)—a work in which the spirit of the Malayalam original is retained.

We have tried to overcome the handicap of literalism that is every translator's bane and have tried to create a bridge between the literary experience of the Malayalam text and the English translation. We have retained Indian words wherever we felt that the word was unsubstitutable in English. In places where we could not render the nuances of the tribal Malayalam idiom and tonality in English, we have re-created the translation to the best of our ability and have been careful to avoid distortions in this narrative, which is so very culture- and context-specific.

We have used kinship terms in many places like '*ayyan*', '*amma*' and '*pannadi*' without translating them because we felt that they conveyed a sense of Mayilamma's world. We have also retained certain forms of address like '*endi*' and '*dei*' because they convey the entire register of emotions from affection to dislike and sarcasm. We have refrained from translating the names of local plants and fishes like '*kummitukeera*' and '*moyyu*' since we felt that the bioregional flavour would be lost in providing genus and species names in English. We have tried to provide interpolations in a non-invasive manner as far as possible. However, we have also provided a comprehensive glossary keeping in mind the general reader.

Mayilamma: The Life of a Tribal Eco-Warrior is not merely the 'atrocity narrative' of an oppressed tribal community but rather a synecdochal, planetary narrative that connects the local pillage of Plachimada's natural resources with other similar environmental struggles by the disenfranchised poor happening throughout the world. The main objective of this English translation, therefore, is to help Mayilamma's narrative secure a place in international environmental justice writing – a place that it richly deserves.

July 2016

Swarnalatha Rangarajan
Sreejith Varma

INTRODUCTION

Mayilamma's Story: The Oiko-autobiography of Self and Place

The English translation, *Mayilamma: The Life of a Tribal Eco-Warrior*, seeks to bring an important regional text in Malayalam, *Mayilamma: Oru Jeevitham* (2012) by Jothibai Pariyadath into the domain of international environmental justice writing. Mayilamma (1940–2007) was an illiterate adivasi woman whose iconic leadership of the local community against the unrestrained extraction and subsequent pollution of water by the multinational giant Coca-Cola has put the nondescript village of Plachimada in Palakkad district of north-central Kerala in India on the map of environmental activism.

Although green slogans like 'Think locally, act globally' have encouraged people to think about the complex, global consequences of their actions, the dialectic connection between the rootedness in the local and a sense of belonging to the global ecosystem is best intuited through life narratives like *Mayilamma* since this life story translates the mantra of ecology ('everything is connected') into a web of concrete relations that includes not only the ecological, but also the cultural, economic and political processes. The manner in which an adivasi woman's life is rhizomatically enmeshed in the rich cultural material of oral lore and tradition as well as the politics of water wars throws open a more expansive understanding of the word 'environment'. The ecological thought that we see in this text is contextual thinking since explaining things in terms of their contexts is really about explaining them in terms of their environment. Redefining the world and reframing the problems of social and environmental justice arise from the ecological concept which Ramachandra Guha and Joan Martinez-Alier refer to as the 'environmentalism of the poor'.

The imbrications of the social and the ecological in Global South environments and the nexus between 'ecology and the politics of survival' (to use the title of Vandana Shiva's 1991 book) pose important questions for environmental justice. Literary texts that emerge from subaltern spaces of developing countries and the toxic environments that influence their creation "suggest the need for new practices of reading both the texts themselves and the place of humans in nature more generally" (Slovic, Rangarajan and Sarveswaran 2015, 3). These texts undertake a unique advocacy by articulating the plight of the 'ecosystem people'—the "stubborn pre-modern survivals in an increasingly post-modern landscape" (Guha 2006, 233)—who rely on the natural resources in their neighbourhood.

Mayilamma's life narrative joins the expanding body of the subaltern 'oiko-autobiographies' in Malayalam. Home ('*oikos*' in Greek) is the fulcrum of these autobiographies which expand to trace the arc of connection from home to the larger home—nature and the surrounding environment comprising both human and other-than-human actors. When the individual self defines its identity through its situatedness in the oikos, the 'self/setting' binary becomes obliterated. The life narratives of these women writers coming from traumatised environments bring the classically underrepresented *oikeion* (a space associated with women, nature and other subalterns) into the public sphere—the *politikon*, thereby establishing a nature-culture continuum between the oikeion and the politikon instead of the customary "opposition" between them (Lyotard 2000, 135). They inspire in the reader the capacity to visualise through an act of participatory reading the attritional 'slow violence' (to use Rob Nixon's term) of fissured earth narratives such as the stories of toxic buildup, water pollution, deforestation, accelerated species loss, and loss of habitats. These stories are often unperceived because they do not explode with cataclysmic violence to grab public attention but, instead, erupt painfully over a long period of time, producing lethal effects in the ecosystem (Nixon 2011). These oiko-autobiographies are repositories of "narrative scholarship" (Slovic 2008, 28) since they offer poignant micronarratives of the self, society, environment and the larger nodal networks of 'ecosickness narratives' (Houser 2014), thereby enabling an emotional comprehension of abstract data. They also advocate a new "partnership ethic" (Merchant 1996, 222) where the connections between local and global governments, economic systems and people are made visible so that new spaces can be forged where basic life needs are enhanced and made secure.

The life narrative of Mayilamma resonates with other oiko-autobiographies emerging from the fissured earthscapes of the Global South and the environmentally traumatised pockets of the North. These writings offer resistance to hegemonic mainstream narrative discourses that obfuscate the violence done to the environment at local and bioregional levels so that this vital information does not invite affirmative action in the form of legislation or monetary compensation (Varma and Rangarajan 2018, 180). *Mayilamma: The Life of a Tribal Eco-Warrior* is comparable to works like *Refuge: An Unnatural History of Family and Place* (1992) by Terry Tempest Williams which presents the author's personal family trauma and her protests against the extensive nuclear testing in the Nevada desert that caused a large number of incidents involving cancer which plagued her family; *Unbowed: A Memoir* (2006) by Wangari Maathai which details how the author countered the repressive Kenyan Government by spearheading the Green Belt Movement to empower local communities and to heal the land that had been ravaged by human greed and ignorance; *Jeevadayini* (2001) [The Life-Giver] by Leelakumariamma which chronicles her long legal battle against the Kerala State Government-owned Plantation Corporation of Kerala (PCK) situated in Kasaragod, which, since 1982, aerially sprayed the carcinogenic pesticide Endosulfan using helicopters, purportedly to protect the cashew crops from 'tea mosquitoes,' seriously affecting human and non-human lives in the predominantly tribal villages around the plantations; *Janu: C.K. Januvinte Jeevitha Katha* (translated into English as *Mother Forest: The Unfinished Story of C. K. Janu*) (2002) that narrates the resistance offered by Janu, a young adivasi woman, who galvanised adivasi support and fought for the restoration of land taken away from them in the name of 'development' following the failure of the Kerala Government to honour its commitment to the adivasis; and *Chengara Samaravum Ente Jeevithavm* [The Chengara Struggle and My Life] (2013), which offers the life-story of Seleena Prakkanam, the Dalit-Christian woman leader of the Chengara land struggle.

Mayilamma's evocation of place and its environmental problem is paradigmatic of micro-scalar agitations that are proliferating elsewhere in India—Kala Dera (Rajasthan), Mehdiganj (Uttar Pradesh) and Gangaikondan (Tamil Nadu), to name a few villages fighting their battles against Coca-Cola. These local struggles and other similar protests against resource extraction that are happening all over the world have environmental justice as a common horizon.

It is ironical that Kerala has been lauded for being closer to the West in terms of social development since the discourse of the acclaimed 'Kerala Model' has ignored the environmental and livelihood risks inherent in these projects. Glaring instances include the pollution of the Chaliyar river in the 1960s owing to pollutants from the Birla Rayon factory, limb deformities and stunted physical growth caused by the aerial spraying of Endosulfan in the state-owned cashew plantations in Kasaragod, and the proposed dam over Kerala's rich rainforests which led to the Silent Valley struggle in the 1970s bringing to the fore issues of ecology.

Mayilamma's life-story is an important text that maps the rise of environmental activism in Kerala, and it weaves into its rhetoric the realities of consumption, globalisation, widening socio-economic inequalities and rising ecological burdens borne by the marginalised poor. Mayilamma's life narrative simply put is that of an earthcarer, from the fringes of the pan-Kerala struggles, who was intensely involved in the protection of livelihoods and local neighbourhoods. Although struggles like Mayilamma's are localised, they seem closer to the environmental justice activism of the '80s in the USA when the focus on justice brought together a group of socially and economically marginalised people of colour into the predominantly white and middle-class environmental movement. Hence the key term that defines these struggles is *environmental justice,* which in turn is linked to struggles for equality and community-wide coalitions between interest groups and class lines. In this new paradigm, the discourses of justice and citizenship as well as the discourses of nature veneration and care come together. In a typical David-Goliath kind of struggle, Mayilamma, a frail, fifty-year old adivasi widow, who fought for the cause of the small village of Plachimada on the Kerala-Tamil Nadu border, became a symbol of the global resistance against Coca-Cola.

The Plachimada Struggle: A David-and-Goliath Story

The social and the environmental are inextricably intertwined in the history of land in Plachimada, a predominantly agricultural area irrigated by the Malampuzha dam with paddy being the dominant crop. Plachimada is a small, economically disadvantaged village which belongs to the Perumatty Panchayat of Kerala's Palakkad district. Most of the villagers are landless adivasis who make their living as agricultural wage labourers. The area is not rain-abundant and is virtually dry during the months of December to March. So it came as a surprise when the Hindustan Coca-Cola Beverages Private Limited (HCBPL) (henceforth referred to as the Company) applied to the Perumatty Panchayat to set up a Bottling Plant in 1999 for which permission was granted in January 2000. There was a lot of speculation about why Coke chose a relatively dry region for its water-based operations. According to the Kerala Sasthra Sahithya Parishad, a voluntary organisation which calls itself the People's Science Movement, Coca-Cola eventually wanted to use water from the irrigation dams close by and also because of Plachimada's proximity to the Palakkad Gap which offered easy access routes to the neighbouring state of Tamil Nadu and the rest of India. According to other sources, American satellite reports identified Plachimada as a land rich in ground water reserves (Nair 2006).

With the diminishing supply of water after the Bottling Plant began operations, paddy fields were utilised to grow less-water-sensitive crops like coconut or allowed to lie fallow. This made the life of the adivasis and Dalits difficult since they were landless and deprived of agricultural wage labour, in addition to being estranged from their traditional ways of life. So when the Plant sucked up all the village water and most of the local wells went dry, the movement took on a distinct ecofeminist tenor since the adivasi women now had to trek long distances in the summer months in search of water.

The Plant required fifteen lakh litres of water on an average per day and its needs were met from diverse sources. Six deep borewells were dug near the factory premises in addition to two deep wells for which the Company paid a low water cess. The 2002 issue of *Down to Earth*, an environmental magazine, alerted readers that the chemical analysis of water samples revealed that limits and parameters regarding extraction of groundwater had been flagrantly breached at Plachimada, and pointed out that high electrical conductivity was the reason for the deterioration of water quality in this area. Also, the recycled wastewater that was used for gardening contained high quantities of carbon dioxide that charged the soil water, resulting in carbonic acid formation which made the water unfit for both human consumption and agricultural use. The solid waste from the Plant was only partially treated and the foul-smelling substance was dumped in landfills or distributed as fertiliser to neighbouring farmers. The seepage of this noxious substance caused contamination in the irrigation canals and soil and also led to rashes and other severe skin problems for farmers who were handling it.

Villagers living in the vicinity of the Plant complained that they could not cook using the water or have a bath since it produced a burning sensation on the skin. The villages around the Plant experienced not just contamination of water but also severe ground water depletion. They claimed that all the nine wells in the Colony became unusable. The worst affected were the economically disadvantaged Colonies where Scheduled Castes and Scheduled Tribes lived such as Plachimada, Vijayanagar, Vellur and Madhavan Nair Colonies of the Perumatty Panchayat, and the Rajeev Nagar and Thothichipathy Colonies of the Pattanchery Panchayat (Nair 2006).

A visit by British journalist John Waite to the HCBPL Plant in 2002 for the 'Face the Facts' programme on BBC Radio 4 proved fortuitous because Waite collected water and sludge samples and got them analysed in a lab operated by the University of Exeter. The lab reports showed high levels of toxic heavy metals, namely cadmium and lead which are carcinogenic, and lethal developmental toxins. The Kerala Pollution Control Board also found dangerous quantities of cadmium in the sludge samples. The Centre for Science and Environment in New Delhi announced that it had found high levels of pesticide in Coke and Pepsi.

The protest which gathered momentum after the disclosure of these facts culminated in a historic march undertaken by adivasi women to the Coca-Cola Plant on Earth Day 22 April 2002 under the aegis of the Adivasi Samrakshana Sangham (Organisation for the Protection of the Adivasis), and the ensuing *satyagraha* which was subjected to harsh punitive action by the police. More than two thousand people showed up for the protest outside the Company gates, forming a blockade, and at least fifty villagers kept vigil on a daily basis in a thatched roof structure—the protest pandal—erected outside the gates.

The Plachimada Struggle or the Plachimada Movement as it is known today is one of the most successful contemporary people's movements against predatory transnational corporations. It is connected in spirit with the struggle against Coco-Cola in Colombia and with many ongoing agrarian struggles in Asia (particularly China), Africa and Latin America, which mark the resurgence of the rural against globalisation (Aiyer 2007). At the forefront were the Coca-Cola Virudha Samara Samithi (The Anti-Coca-Cola Struggle Committee) and the Plachimada Solidarity Committee which brought together many social organisations, non-governmental organisations, youth groups and political parties. The Plachimada struggle was a non-violent one despite the atrocities unleashed on adivasi women by the police and arrest warrants issued by the Government in the names of the protesters. Pictures of Gandhi and the Buddha adorned the small protest pandal as people made an emotional connection between Gandhi's satyagraha against colonial rule and the Plachimada struggle against neo-colonial powers. The Plachimada Declaration, in fact, drew upon the vocabulary of the Indian freedom struggle when it proclaimed, "Coca-Cola Pepsi-Cola[1] 'Quit India'" (Chattopadhyay and Franke 2006, 201). According to Gopal, a Gandhian peace activist who was a member of the Kerala Sarvodaya Mandalam, "As long as truth and dharma prevail in the world, they cannot fail" (Parmar 2015, 76).

The agitation drew support from activists in the country and outside and also the attention of the national and international press. Narmada dam activist Medha Patkar started her anti-globalisation *yatra* (journey, march) from Plachimada to voice her protest against Coca-Cola. Another environmental activist, Vandana Shiva, arranged for a World Water Conference in January 2004 in Plachimada, which was attended by water activists like Maude Barlow and Jose Bove. This conference added a new dimension to the epistemology of the Plachimada struggle. It used the term 'water privatisation' to describe the plunder that was taking place. The plethora of activists who had gathered in Plachimada recommended that water should be recognised as part of the public commons, and they advocated the creation of political spaces that encouraged alternative forms of water governance. The Plachimada Declaration that was drafted at the conference stated eloquently: "Water is not a private property. It is a common resource for the sustenance of all ... The right to conserve, use and manage water is fully vested with the local community. This is the very basis of water democracy. Any attempt to reduce or deny this right is a crime" (Chattopadhyay and Franke 2006, 201).

[1] Pepsi-Cola is the earlier (1898–1960) name of present-day Pepsi.

The Perumatty Panchayat refused to renew the Company's licence in March 2003, a decision that was stayed by a State Government order. The High Court ordered the Company to stop drawing groundwater within a month but instructed the Village Council to renew the licence. The following years witnessed a series of legal skirmishes between the Village Council and the Company, and a lot of back-and-forth deliberations between the High Court and the Supreme Court. Significant dates in the history of the protest are: 19 August 2005, the day on which the Kerala State Pollution Control Board ordered the production unit in Plachimada to close down for not complying with pollution control norms; and 10 and 11 August 2006 when the Government of Kerala and the State Food (Health) Authority banned the manufacture and sale of Coca-Cola in the state. The Plachimada Coca-Cola Victims Relief and Compensation Claims Special Tribunal Bill was passed on 24 February 2011 by the Kerala Legislative Assembly. However, bureaucratic procedures have stood in the way of the bill being passed by Parliament. The victims of Plachimada's water plunder cannot claim compensation under the National Green Tribunal Act (2010) due to jurisdictional hassles and the prevalent illiteracy and poverty that prevented them from making a proper representation (Rejitha et al. 2013).

The protest pandal stands as a symbol of a poor tribal community's thousand-plus days' fight for self-governance. The protest upholds a philosophy of life that believes in sharing the resources of nature for subsistence in preference to 'developmental' rapacity and consumption for the sake of profit. Today the protest pandal is deserted but for one Kanniamma, an old tribal woman, who makes it a point to sit in the pandal for some time every day as if to preserve the sacredness of the space and remind the community of its struggle. Mayilamma's humble, unmarked grave amidst the thickets of Plachimada, exposed to the open skies, remains as a poignant reminder of the bare lives of the poor.

The course of the Plachimada struggle that began as a silent vigil by adivasi villagers and soon cascaded into full-blown war fought by actors, both local and international, for the cause of environmental justice jeopardised Coca-Cola's symbolic cultural capital. Coca-Cola had re-entered the Indian market in 1993 during the post-economic liberalisation era as an emblem of globalisation promising easy availability of consumables to all and a good standard of living, and more importantly as a drink that symbolised American values. However, the "stability of its connotative matrix" degenerated after Plachimada and came to be resemanticised as Killer Coke that spelled drought and destroyed life in Plachimada and other parts of rural India (Ghosh 2010, 359). Coke denied the allegations, tried to publicise its lab results, and employed Bollywood icon Aamir Khan as a brand ambassador to endorse the safety of the drink. Coke managed to resuscitate its image after Neville Isdell took over as CEO in June 2004. Speaking at a conference hosted by the World Wildlife Fund in June 2007, Isdell's words indicated the Company's image makeover, "Too many people suffer from lack of drinking water...so we at Coca-Cola Company have placed highest priority on being responsible water users" (Pendergrast 2013, 449–50).

However, this David-Goliath fight for environmental justice has yielded only a partial victory since financial reparation for the adivasi protesters is yet to be realised.

Towards Earth Democracy: From the Oikeion to the Politikon

Mayilamma's life narrative reveals a unique space of advocacy which blends radical and Gandhian elements to form a new earth ethic to acknowledge the simultaneity of negotiation and protest, the importance of bioregional dwelling and community-based action. The 'I' in Mayilamma's oiko-autobiography is not an 'enclosed self' but an emplaced subjectivity since the autobiographical act of this book also substitutes the customary tripartite (self, life, writing) structure with land, memory, and stories (Allister 2001). The author's identity in the narrative, in other words, is intricately bound up with the author's location, Plachimada. The book records a community's ecological dispossession, when the community-control over a common resource like water is first transferred to the state which is then passed on to corporate powers, thus driving a previously self-sufficient local community into a marathon struggle for water democracy and sustainable livelihood.

Mayilamma's intimate recollections of her childhood days that are embedded in the forest and the traditional season-based organic agricultural practices come as temporal breaks in the narrative. These pastoral vignettes help to heighten the poignancy of the descriptions of the abject environmental conditions of present-day Plachimada and the trauma suffered by its inhabitants. This holistic thinking, as is evident from Mayilamma's life narrative, emanates from the close-knit nature of her tribal community. She describes how the womenfolk get together in the afternoons to listen to the old clan stories narrated by the tribal elder, Pappal. This is a space which is not binarised by gender since the congregation is also joined by men who are out of work. These informal social gatherings, in addition to the occasional *oorukoottams*, serve as platforms for handing down the community lore, customs and histories to the younger generations.

The early chapters of Mayilamma's life narrative offer fascinating glimpses into the tribal way of life. Mayilamma belongs to a tribal community called 'Eravallar' (Tamil for 'inhabitants of the hilly tracts'). It is estimated that there are about thirty-eight tribal communities in Kerala, the majority of whom are concentrated in the districts of Wayanad, Idukki, Palakkad and Kottayam. The Eravallar tribals are also known as Eravallan, Irula, Erukala, Irava, Irular and Iruliga. They are found in the Annamalai hills of the Western Ghats and are assumed to have migrated from Coimbatore (Tamil Nadu) to Kerala where they settled in places like Vellimedu, Kannimari, Attayampathy and Chemmanampathy in the Chittur taluk of Palakkad. The mother tongue of the Eravallars is 'Eravalla', an endangered language. To outsiders and sometimes even to their own community members, they speak in Tamil, a language which they are fluent in (Gnanasundaram, Vijayan and Suresh 2014). In Chapter Thirteen, Mayilamma explains how listening to numerous public speeches and her own interactions with others have helped her to pick up more Malayalam words so that she "could switch to Malayalam if occasion demanded". Plenty of Tamil words are used in the original text. Most of the kinship terms like *'ayyan,' 'annan,' 'atha,' 'pannadi'* and *'moraimaman'* that Mayilamma uses are markedly Tamil. A few of the folk songs included in the text are, as is customary with the Eravallars, narrated in Tamil (Gnanasundaram, Vijayan and Suresh 2014). The vocal rendering of these folk songs is an indispensable part of the Eravallar rituals, especially those pertaining to marriage and death.

The songs, drumbeats, rituals and dances mentioned through the course of this narrative can be classified as the composite elements of a ceremonial way of life whose purpose is not self-expression but an immersion in community and the idea of the inter-relatedness of all life. For instance, the idol of the elephant god, Pillaiyar, which is made out of cow dung during the harvest season, is immersed in water after the festivities are over. There is a recognition of and reverence for materiality in this culture. Devices like the reiteration of 'meaningless' syllables are employed in lullabies, laments and marriage songs throughout the text. These songs convey a plethora of emotions: they tease, praise, describe, lament and offer ritual adoration. They portray other-than-humans as relatives, as is common in all tribal systems. For example, the palmyra is addressed using a kinship term like 'sister' in Chapter Nine and is constructed as an important player in the song who calls out to Pillaiyar. These ceremonies may be enacted before people who do not play an active role, but the chief objective is participation, attention and being attuned to the activities and needs of the community members (Allen 1996).

The ceremonial songs in the 'oikic' part of this life narrative include songs of marriage, of mourning, of planting, harvesting and other nature-culture cycles which keep the clan together and knit the human with the world of nature. One can detect, as in Sangam *tinai* (genre, type) ecopoetics, a kind of oikic continuity between landscape, clan deity and the nature of emotions. The narrative seamlessly integrates Mayilamma and her friends while at work in the fields, recounting the story of the Tamil god, Velavar, who wooed Valli by shooing away birds in the millet fields. A strong environmental ethic emerges from the story when Mayilamma says that their clan would never chop the kino tree because in the story Lord Velavar changed himself into a kino tree to escape the wrath of Valli's brothers. The same preservation ethic is extended to the peacock, which is the vehicle of Lord Velavar according to mythology.

There is an organic rootedness in the processes of nature in every social aspect of tribal life. For example, the *thali*, which is traditionally a flat piece of gold suspended from a yellow thread or a golden chain that the groom ties around the bride's neck on the wedding day, is a seed of the castor tree. After the groom ties it, the village elders sing a couple of folk songs that ensure entertainment appropriate for the festive occasion while they also act as a timely reminder to the husband about his marital obligations. Similarly, the excerpts from the *oppari* songs that are included in the text are part of the death ceremonies in the Tamil folk tradition when women beat their breasts and sing these story-songs to mourn the death of a relative. The mourning song for a departed female elder in Chapter Fifteen employs the language of ecofeminism. Although the initial focus of this lament is the oleander bush with bright flowers planted by the departed soul, it eventually employs a master metaphor wherein the departed woman is described as a shade-giving plant.

The songs sung during different phases of cultivation such as the planting of seedlings and harvesting typically contain rhythmic refrains and reflect the master–labourer relationships in the traditional feudal system where, for example, the event of the coming of the overseer is expressed with fear. These songs gave expression to their joys and sorrows and singing them was a way of forgetting their hunger and backbreaking toil in the fields from dawn to dusk. The influence of Tamil culture is also evident in the rituals around the celebration of a girl reaching puberty. Placing a bow and arrow is an indispensable part of most of the Eravallar ceremonies including female puberty rituals and marriage. The text is also a rich mine of information regarding indigenous medical practices using herbs for treatments ranging from fever and chest congestion to childbirths and postnatal mother care, age-old rituals like the seclusion of new mothers and menstruating women in a separate hut, and the tribal food culture. The Eravallar cuisine is typically non-vegetarian and includes a variety of dishes made from ragi, *chama,* tapioca, different kinds of spinach and wild tubers, crab, local fish varieties like *paral, chodiyan* and *moyyu* and spices like pepper, cumin seeds and turmeric. The narrative includes elaborate accounts of crab hunting and instructions on how to cook fish, crabs, spinach and tubers. The horse gram harvest season is also described with great enthusiasm. The reason for this jubilation is explained using the stark logic of the poor: "If we had corn rice and stewed horse gram once a day, we could easily let go of food for the rest of the day." These passages in the text bring to the forefront the issue of food sovereignty[2] which is becoming problematic for most tribal communities throughout the world. As traditional wild food landscapes dwindle, these communities which are totally dependent on local resources suffer immensely.

The oikeion, however, is not a pristine world of abundance but is mediated by the subaltern status of the tribal. For instance, the *muthalalis* in Mayilamma's life narrative are associated with institutionalised oppression and exploitation of gullible tribals. Mayilamma's life narrative implicates the muthalalis' dishonesty in grabbing the lands that were originally distributed to the tribals by the Kollengode King. These muthalalis appear after the tribal peasants have tilled the lands and made them ready for cultivation and use various tactics ranging from monetary inducements to intimidation, thereby snatching the land and the fruits of their labour. Mayilamma narrates how her people were diminished to the state where they did not have even a burial ground and had to cross the border to bury

[2] Food sovereignty is the right of people to healthy and culturally appropriate food produced through ecologically sound and sustainable methods, and their right to define their own food and agriculture systems.

their dead in the Gounders' land in Tamil Nadu. This often resulted in open confrontation between the tribals and the Gounders. She indicates how the muthalalis disapproved of tribal children going to school since it would mean fewer field hands. Mayilamma also recounts how the muthalali had tried to prevent her and her siblings from going to school. However, the tribals, asserts Mayilamma, have come to realise that their lack of education is the prime reason for their oppressed state and that they now see to it that their children go to school and get educated. This is also true in the case of Mayilamma herself. After her husband Marimuthu's premature death, his mother had tried to persuade Mayilamma to remarry. Many people had also approached her parents seeking her hand in marriage. But she was resolute in her decision not to marry again for the sake of her sons whom she was determined to send to school.

The passage from the oikeion to the politikon in Mayilamma's life narrative is presented as a continuum rather than as an abrupt transition from the private to the public sphere. In Chapter Eleven of the narrative, while describing her husband's death, Mayilamma declares: "That is how this Mayilamma entered into life's battle at the age of twenty-seven." The metaphor of a 'battle' becomes the defining word for her personal as well as public life. It was her battle with tribal illiteracy and backwardness that made her protect the interests of tribal children who went to the Anganwadi school where they were assured of one square meal a day and basic literacy. The opening chapter of the narrative focuses on the gruel cooked in contaminated water, and Mayilamma's concern for the children who have fallen ill.

This ecosickness narrative is primarily one of hope. Mayilamma draws on the David and Goliath story to visualise the light at the end of the tunnel: "One of the leaders told us a Christian story. The story of a boy named David who defeated a giant called Goliath. Our fight with the Company was similar to this story! They told us that in the story it was the boy who won the fight. We thought that we, like him, would also win the battle even if it took a long time."

It is this optimism and spirit of fearlessness that transforms this illiterate adivasi woman into a fiery public speaker. The Plachimada protest pandal becomes the intersection where the home and the world meet and a symbol of the 'sacramental commons' where "people as individuals and communities concretize ecological ethics in local contexts" (Hart 2006, 200). Mayilamma's battle upholds the sanctity of water not merely as a bioregional commons, but also as an earth commons.

Her activism brings to the forefront issues that threaten most tribal societies in India like the loss of local knowledge, loss of identity and displacement due to faulty measures by the state that jettison these cultures into the widening arc of economic development and modernity.

Mayilamma questions this lopsided development and defines freedom as unrestricted access to land, water and air. The absence of these vital elements indicated a state of slavery as far as she was concerned. She raises a pertinent question: "Will eating sweets, planting the flag and shouting 'Jai Jai' mean freedom?"

On becoming the recipient of the prestigious Speak Out Award and Sthree Shakti Award, Mayilamma's world expanded from Plachimada to India's capital city where she got to meet important politicians like Sonia Gandhi. However, this glittering political arena is always informed by the oikic as far as Mayilamma is concerned. She confesses that she had just one thing to tell leaders like Sonia Gandhi: "There is a small well in front of my house. We were drinking water all these days from that well. Now the water is not good. We are not against you giving any company a permit or an award. But can you bring the good water back to our well?"

Mayilamma's narrative ends on a cautionary note and resonates in spirit with the speech attributed to Chief Seattle, a nineteenth-century American Indian chief of the Duwamish tribe. If Seattle speaks of the "end of living and the beginning of survival" (Rothenberg 1999, 36), Mayilamma points out with a sense of fatigue that this is not the first time that the earth has been ravished. Speaking of the Plachimada struggle she says, "We will be happy if it ends well. We will take it as a deserving reward for our fight. On the other hand, if we lose the struggle, the story of Plachimada will remain a lesson to all."

Mayilamma's words speak to the history of environmental disasters in India like the Bhopal Gas Tragedy (1984), pollution of life-giving rivers like the Ganga and the Yamuna, ill-conceived mega dams that spawn developmental refugees and man-made floods, shrinking of the commons, nuclear contamination and a host of other problems. Oiko-autobiographies like *Mayilamma* strongly critique environmental practices that target the poor and the vulnerable and make a strong plea for justice by demanding that environmental burdens and rewards be shared equally by all irrespective of creed, caste, colour or gender. This narrative brings home the need to strive for "earth democracy" (to use Vandana Shiva's phrase), "the ecological security that the earth provides, and the social security that we create through community" (Shiva 2005, 184).

July 2016

Swarnalatha Rangarajan
Sreejith Varma

References

Aiyer, Ananthakrishnan. 2007. 'The Allure of the Transnational: Notes on Some Aspects of the Political Economy of Water in India.' *Cultural Anthropology* 22: 640–58. Accessed 4 July 2016. doi: 10.1525/can.2007.22.4.640.

Allister, Mark. 2001. *Refiguring the Map of Sorrow: Nature Writing and Autobiography*. Charlottesville: University Press of Virginia.

Allen, Paula Gunn. 1996. 'The Sacred Hoop: A Contemporary Perspective.' In *The Ecocriticism Reader: Landmarks in Literary Ecology*, edited by Cheryll Glotfelty and Harold Fromm, 241–64. Athens: University of Georgia Press.

Bhaskaran. 2002. *Janu: C. K. Januvinte Jeevitha Katha*. Kottayam: DC Books.

_____. 2004. *Mother Forest: The Unfinished Story of C. K. Janu*. Translated by N. Ravi Shankar. New Delhi: Women Unlimited and Kali for Women.

Chattopadhyay, Srikumar, and Richard W. Franke. 2006. *Striving for Sustainability: Environmental Stress and Democratic Initiatives in Kerala*. New Delhi: Concept Publishing Company.

Ghosh, Bishnupriya. 2010. 'Looking through Coca-Cola: Global Icons and the Popular.' *Public Culture* 22: 333–68. Accessed 4 July 2016. doi: 10.1215/08992363-2009-031.

Gnanasundaram, V, N. Vijayan, and P. Suresh. 2014. 'On Eravalla.' *International Journal of Dravidian Linguistics* 38: 1–3. Accessed 4 July 2016. <http://www.ijdl.org/html/NOV_14.pdf>

Guha, Ramachandra. 2006. *How Much Should a Person Consume? Environmentalism in India and the United States*. London: University of California Press.

Guha, Ramachandra, and Joan Martinez-Alier. 1997. *Varieties of Environmentalism: Essays North and South*. London: Earthscan Publications.

Hart, John. 2006. *Sacramental Commons: Christian Ecological Ethics*. Lanham, MD: Rowman and Littlefield.

Houser, Heather. 2014. *Ecosickness in Contemporary US Fiction*. New York: Columbia University Press.

Leelakumariamma. 2011. *Jeevadayini*. Transcribed by T. Ajeesh. Kottayam: DC Books.

Lyotard, Jean-François. 2000. 'Ecology as Discourse of the Secluded.' In *The Green Studies Reader: From Romanticism to Ecocriticism*, edited by Laurence Coupe, 135–38. London: Routledge.

Maathai, Wangari Muta. 2006. *Unbowed: A Memoir*. New York: Knopf.

Mayilamma. 2012. *Mayilamma: Oru Jeevitham*. Transcribed by Jothibai Pariyadath. Kozhikode: Mathrubhumi Books.

Merchant, Carolyn. 1996. *Earthcare: Women and the Environment*. New York: Routledge.

Nair, D. V. Muraleedharan. 2006. 'Whose Water? A Study of the Struggle for Water at Plachimada, Kerala.' *Studies in Humanities and Social Sciences* 13: 1–14. Accessed 4 July 2016. <http://www.inflibnet.ac.in/ojs/index.php/SHSS/article/view/3192/2473>

Nixon, Rob. 2011. *Slow Violence and the Environmentalism of the Poor*. Cambridge, MA: Harvard University Press.

'Now, Cola-Water War.' 2002. *Down to Earth*, August 15. Accessed 4 July 2016. <http://www.downtoearth.org.in/news/now-colawater-war-14971>

Parmar, Pooja. 2015. *Indigeneity and Legal Pluralism in India: Claims, Histories, Meanings*. New York: Cambridge University Press.

Pendergrast, Mark. 2013. *For God, Country and Coca-Cola: The Definitive History of the Great American Soft Drink and the Company That Makes It*. New York: Basic Books.

Pokkudan, Kallen. 2010. *Ente Jeevitham*. Transcribed by Sreejith Paithalen. Kottayam: DC Books.

______. 2010. *Kandalkkadukalkkidayil Ente Jeevitham*, edited by Thaha Madayi. Kottayam: DC Books.

Prakkanam, Seleena. 2013. *Chengara Samaravum Ente Jeevithavum*. Transcribed by O. K. Santhosh and M. B. Manoj. Kottayam: DC Books.

Rejitha, V. P. Roshini, Glitereena, and Rahamath. 2013. 'Road to Plachimada.' *Centre for Economy, Development and Law*. Accessed 4 July 2016. <http://www.cedl.ac.in/wp-content/uploads/2015/03/plachimada-bill-2011-1.pdf>

Rothenberg, David. 1999. 'Will the Real Chief Seattle Please Speak Up? An Interview with Ted Perry.' In *The New Earth Reader: The Best of Terra Nova*, edited by David Rothenberg and Martha Ulveaus, 36–51. Cambridge, MA: MIT Press.

Shiva, Vandana. 2005. *Earth Democracy: Justice, Sustainability, and Peace*. London: Zed Books.

______. 1991. *Ecology and the Politics of Survival: Conflicts over Natural Resources in India*. Newbury Park, CA: Sage.

Slovic, Scott. 2008. *Going Away to Think: Engagement, Retreat, and Ecocritical Responsibility*. Reno: University of Nevada Press.

Slovic, Scott, Swarnalatha Rangarajan, and Vidya Sarveswaran. 2015. 'Introduction.' In *Ecocriticism of the Global South*, edited by Scott Slovic, Swarnalatha Rangarajan, and Vidya Sarveswaran, 1–10. Lanham: Lexington Books.

Varma, Sreejith, and Swarnalatha Rangarajan. 2018. 'The Politics of Land, Water and Toxins: Reading the Life-narratives of Three Women Oikos-carers from Kerala.' In *Women and Nature? Beyond Dualism in Gender, Body, and Environment*, edited by Douglas Vakoch and Sam Mickey, 167–84. New York: Routledge.

Williams, Terry Tempest. 1992. *Refuge: An Unnatural History of Family and Place*. New York: Vintage Books.

THE PLACHIMADA STORY

A Time Line

1998:	HCCBPL acquires 34.4 acres of land to set up a Bottling Plant in Plachimada.
25 January 2000:	Perumatty Panchayat issues licence to start production.
March 2000:	Operations commence in the Plant.
22 April 2002:	Protest against the Company commences led by the 'Coca-Cola Virudha Samara Samithi' (henceforth Samithi).
7 June 2002:	The Samithi leads a 500-member rally.
4 August 2002:	The Samithi organises a rally of over a 1000.
7 April 2003:	Perumatty Panchayat refuses to renew licence.
12 June 2003:	Local Self-Government Department (LSD) of the State Government stays the Panchayat decision.
25 July 2003:	BBC Radio 4 programme 'Face the Facts' reports the presence of carcinogens in the waste deposited by the Plant.
7 August 2003:	The Kerala State Pollution Control Board (KSPCB) confirms BBC report and orders Coke to recover all waste and store it in safe containment.
16 December 2003:	Single judge bench of the Kerala High Court upholds the Panchayat's decision.

23 January 2004:	Three-day World Water Conference organised in Plachimada. Plachimada Declaration issued.
12 February 2004:	High Court division bench allows Company to extract water till this date.
21 February 2004:	Government of Kerala declares Palakkad District to be drought affected.
9 March 2004:	Company stops operations.
15 January 2005:	1000th day of the protest.
12 February 2005:	Committee set up by High Court submits report stating maximum permissible usage of water must not exceed 5,00,000 litres per day.
22 April 2005:	Huge rally organised at Plachimada to mark three years of protest.
1 June 2005:	High Court issues ultimatum to Panchayat to grant licence; three-month licence issued subject to strict regulations.
19 August 2005:	KSPCB rejects Company's application stating that heavy metal cadmium concentration was 400 to 600% above the tolerance limit. Company asked to stop production.
16 November 2005:	High Court again demands that the Perumatty Panchayat issue a licence.
19 November 2005:	Water Resource Department includes Plachimada under the category "overexploited".
November 2005:	Panchayat files SLP in Supreme Court against the latest High Court order.
January 2006:	Company begins considering moving operations away from Plachimada.
30 June 2010:	Chief Minister V. S. Achuthanandan announces the State Cabinet's decision to

	set up a dedicated legal agency to assess compensation due to every applicant.
16 February 2011:	State Cabinet approves a draft bill, passed shortly thereafter in the Legislative Assembly, to form a tribunal for securing compensation.
23 February 2011:	Plachimada Coca-Cola Victims Relief and Compensation Claims Special Tribunal Bill 2011 passed.
December 2014:	Centre directs State to approach National Green Tribunal (NGT).
4 February 2016:	President of India returns the Bill.
12 June 2016:	Kerala Home Department registers a criminal case against Coca-Cola invoking provisions of Scheduled Castes and Scheduled Tribes (Prevention of Atrocities) Act, 1989, for groundwater exploitation and pollution in Plachimada.

Main Source of Information

Mathews, Rohan D. 2011. 'The Plachimada Struggle against Coca-Cola in Southern India.' *Ritmo.org*, Accessed July 12, 2016. <https://www.ritimo.org/The-Plachimada-Struggle-against-Coca-Cola-in-Southern-India>

MAYILAMMA

The Life of a Tribal Eco-Warrior

ONE

Premonition

In the morning while I was drying my saree on the clothes line in the outer yard after taking a dip in the Kambalathara lake, I heard loud voices drifting from the *Anganwadi*. It was the beginning of the *Kumbha* month. The summer heat had already set in. I wondered how long we would have to wait for at least two good rains that would put an end to the water scarcity of the summer months. Having a bath did not help because the water in the lake was muddy and the foul odour from the moss stuck to the clothes even after they dried. My elder son Murugan's woman, Lechumi, would comment, "It seems that this well water is not enough for *amma*. She feels happy only when she takes a dip in that dirty pond."

She was right. This was a habit of mine that has persisted from childhood. Even if the well water had been as clear as teardrops, I would still bathe only in the pond. Drawing water from the well with a mud pot and having a bath was, to me, a poor way of going about it. Bathing in this manner did not give me any satisfaction.

The commotion near the Anganwadi was increasing. The loudest voice that I could hear was that of Selvi, my neighbour Pappathi's granddaughter. I think it was helper Chella who was talking to her, giving back as much as she got.

I abandoned the remaining clothes on the line to go and investigate. People had gathered near the foot of the neem tree in the outer courtyard. There was utter confusion. Rohini teacher, who was new to the place, looked frightened and kept her distance from the din.

"*Endi*, why do people like you come to work? If you can't use clean water to make rice gruel, why are you in this job? What do you think you are doing if you can't even boil rice properly? Go away! This is no place for you to work!"

Somehow I calmed Selvi down and asked her what the matter was.

"Tell me, Mayilatha, are the ayah and the teacher doing such a tough job? They have not cleaned the rice well or boiled the gruel properly. All the kids here are suffering from severe stomach ache. If they can't do the work properly, why don't they leave? That is what I was trying to tell them!"

What Selvi said was right. Yesterday two or three children in the Colony were down with diarrhoea. I heard my daughter Deivana complaining about it this morning. She said that for some time now her tummy did not feel quite all right after eating.

Even the grownups seemed to have the same problem. The gruel and rice have been tasting bitter for quite some time. However long the *dal* is boiled, it just does not seem to cook. Was it something to do with the water? But how was this possible? We have been cooking for so many years using the same water. It is not just us, the people of Plachimada Colony have also been using water from the same Panchayat well for cooking and drinking.

It looked as though Selvi would not keep quiet. She was creating a hullabaloo. I got angry. The girl simply would not understand. The new teacher was standing there, frightened, but Chella was unfazed. Chella came here from Vandithavalam to work as an ayah sixteen years ago. She supplemented her job by acting in plays. Whenever I had some leisure I would go to the Anganwadi. Chella would introduce me to plays and songs. She would sing and play out the roles of Sheelavathy, Savithri and Chandramathy.

"Please don't worry. Let them prepare the rice gruel themselves for two days. They will realise that the fault was not yours," I told Chella and the teacher.

The mothers of the Anganwadi children were muttering under their breath that there was truth to what Selvi and the others were saying. Although I had mediated the dispute for the time being, my mind was still not at peace. Something in me told me that there was a problem. The others did not speak about it, but I knew that they were also nagged by the same doubt.

It was only after many days that all of us in the Colony came to know what the problem really was.

TWO

Coca-Cola Arrives in Plachimada

The Grama Sabha would meet once in five or six months in Perumatty. Usually it was the members and promoters who got to attend the meeting. Nobody would bother calling us. The member would come back and share the decisions taken in the meeting. At that point of time, Bhaskarettan was the member in Ward Five of Vijayanagar Colony. One day when we met he said, "Mayilamma, a big company is going to be set up in our ward. All your toiling in the mud and slush will be lessened considerably if it happens. If nothing else, you will be able to work without being exposed to the sun and rain. Some of you will also get jobs."

I told him right then, "That is not right, Bhaskaretta! If the company comes to our place, we will be ruined! It is being brought here to destroy all our water!"

There was a reason why I said this because I had heard something like that before. There was a Soya company in a place called Amrampalayam in Tamil Nadu, ten kilometres from this place. One of our men went to work there. Four or five borewells were drilled on the company land for water. Here one has to dig only a few feet to find water. Since the company was located on higher ground, the machine had to dig much deeper there. What do you think the machine did? It sucked dry all the water from the neighbouring canals. So what did it all amount to? The land which once produced two harvests of rice, corn, sorghum and millets did not even yield one now because there was no water. Drought arrived in those places. This is what an educated Gounder who worked in that company told our man. He said that the place was destroyed because of the company. That is why we were all gripped by fear when the member told us that the company was coming to our place. Seeing how frightened we were, the member told us: "Such things will not happen here. Even if there is going to be water scarcity, we will find a way. We will bring water through tankers, pipes—whatever. Let the company come first. What is more important is jobs for our people. Even if all this comes to nothing, it is still a matter of pride for our Panchayat that we are going to get such a big company!"

He said this to us the other day and made us shut our mouths. Poor man, he died all of a sudden after six months. After that the Colony was put under Ward Eight.[3] When we asked Ward Member Varadettan about this, he shrugged it off. I do not think that the Panchayat met after that.

Afterwards, the *oorukoottam* would meet in the Anganwadi. When Promoter Muthulachumi issued the notice, we would go to attend.

Not that there would be lengthy discussions. People would talk about ration cards, roofing for their huts and *patta* titles. Everybody gathered there would bring up their own problems. Sometimes heads nodded to say yes and at other times to say no. Either way, I felt that no good was coming the way of our people.

It was certain that the Company would come. We thought that nothing would happen as we had feared. Would our Government do anything that could harm us? In any case we also punched our votes for them! Also it was not right on our part to create obstacles in the matter of jobs for our people. What if they point a finger at us tomorrow for halting the country's progress? So we kept mum.

The Company finally arrived. If you ask if our people got jobs, they surely did. The job of cleaning bottles! What could we tell them when they asked us what other job could be given

[3] According to the Plachimada High Power Committee Report published in 2010, the Plachimada area comprised Wards 4, 8 and 9 with a total area of 14.51 square kilometres.

to uneducated and simple people like us? About seven or eight of us turned up for that job too!

Once the Company opened, there was noise all day and all night. Lorries kept coming and going. We got to understand that what was manufactured there were bottles filled with some sort of drinking water. The kids said that the boozers used to mix it with toddy and drink it. One day when I was suffering from stomach pain, shopkeeper Nataraja Gounder's wife said, "Mayilamma, drinking Cola is good for gas trouble." That's how, by paying ten rupees, I bought myself a bottle of Cola and drank it. I felt as if something was burning down my intestines.

Some four or five weeks had passed since the Company had started. I thought our fears were misplaced. The water in the well had not lessened. Rather, it seemed to have increased. We wondered how this could have happened. To tell the truth, we outsiders do not have a clue about what is going on inside the Company. Back then, and now. When the water level rose in our wells, we thought that no borewell had been drilled here as in the Soya company's grounds.

We came to know the truth of this only later.

THREE

Living in the Lap of the Forest

Due to their advanced age, two grandmothers were considered to be the most important people of our Colony. Both of them had the same name. Pappal. One of them died last year after the protest started. The other one who is alive is Pappal of Pulianthoppu. She is an aunt of sorts to me. Sometimes the womenfolk would gather after midday. *Pappammayi* would entertain us with old stories. The menfolk who were jobless would also keep dropping in and out to listen to her. *Ammayi* did not know what her exact age was. If you asked her she would retort, "How am I to know? My father and mother are dead!"

Like me, Pappammayi was also brought to Perumatty after marriage. In those days there were no roads, houses or Colonies. The land all the way from Kanyakumari to Meenakshipuram was the property of the Kollengode king. The king distributed the property as he wished to people of his choice. They were the landlords. Lazy bones, all of them! Too lazy to woo the forest and till the land, they gave it away to the *adivasis*. In those days, the forest spread up to the Eastern hills. It was home to bears, elephants and leopards.

Wooing the forest is not an easy job. Clearing the undergrowth and setting it on fire, felling the big trees, chopping their trunks and digging up their roots, building ridges and making the soil ready for agriculture were back-breaking tasks. No landlord would pay any attention until the forest was cleared and made ready. They would come after it was transformed into fields and thickets. They were mainly the Tamil Gounders.They would slowly strike up a friendship

IMAGE 1: Mayilamma with Jothibai Pariyadath.

Source: Courtesy, *Mathrubhumi* archives.

with our men. Then they would engage in glib talk: "*Dei*, Vella, the spot of land where I am standing is good. Why don't you give it to me? I will take care of it!"

Poor Vella. He would try protesting at first. He must have worked like a fiend to clear a tiny bit of the forest. He earned his daily gruel from selling the dug-up roots and wood chips from the forest. There was no point in protesting. He would only get beaten up. They would enter his hovel and throw out all the pots and pans. However, if he kept silent he would get a hundred or two hundred rupees. Either way, the land on which he had laboured so hard was sure to leave his hands.

Pappammayi had seen many such things in her life and suffered many losses. She had six children. Four of them had houses of their own. Pazhanimala *annan*, Pappammayi's elder sister's son, lived with her. Annan's wife and children were dead. Pappammayi's youngest son was somewhat well off and worked in a toddy shop. Pappammayi assisted the childbirths of almost all the girls in the Colony. She did not approve of people going to hospitals to get treatment. If anybody tried to update her with stories of the present, she would retort, "It was not so in our time." Ammayi herself took care of the health needs of the new mothers and babies. In those days what medicine was available? She would feed the new mothers an extract of pepper essence twice a day. She often claimed there was no better medicine than pepper that could heal the rawness in a new mother's stomach. In the good old days when Pappammayi came to Perumatty, her people worked for Mathavan *Moothar* of Kannimari. Later they lost their lands because of debts and law suits. It was then that they were given *micha bhoomi*—the surplus land. Her family was the first to arrive in the Colony.

Back in those days when they first came, there was a huge lake where the Company building stands today. *Neeluri* shrubs grew abundantly on the shore of the lake and the expanse of these indigo thickets spread far and wide into the area beyond. I too remember seeing all this when I came here after my marriage. Pappammayi narrated how she went to the neeluri thicket to relieve herself, but ran away in fear when she found herself looking into the unblinking eyes of a leopard.

In those days we did not have anything to eat when we were out to clear the forest. When we dug up the soil, we would find a variety of tuber; we called it *noolankizhangu*. Its roots would travel down to a man's height. To get one of these, we would dig the earth, make steps to climb down into the pit and cull the tuber. A single tuber steamed with a pinch of salt was good enough to feed ten to twelve people.

The forest had plenty of medicinal herbs. Pappammayi was familiar with all of them. Whenever we caught a fever or cold, she would light a fire using stones and drop *thumba* leaves and castor leaves in water and make us inhale the steam. The fever would flee in no time. Pappammayi looked after my grandchildren as well. She was a woman who believed in cleanliness. In those days women were isolated in special huts during their periods, at childbirth and at the onset of puberty. Nowadays there is no such taboo. She would say that people living in a polluted house would lose their eyes and also be deprived of the rice for their daily gruel. If a woman was with child, Pappammayi would see her through all the phases of pregnancy till the child was born. The kids these days do not know anything. Even I do not know all these customs and other matters so well. I go by whatever the elders say. It was during the time of Pappammayi's parents that the ways of the forest came to be replaced by the ways of the city. These days we follow a few customs from Tamil Nadu. We also follow a few others from Kerala.

In those days the bride wore a thali of castor seeds strung on a thread. There is an old story told by grandmothers about a young man who went north in search of a thali and never came back. This is the reason why the people of our community started using the Kerala style thali.

We have similar stories for each and every thing.

FOUR

The Plight of the Adivasis

I have heard that there are about thirty-five different adivasi clans. I do not know all their names. According to the Government records our people come under the Eravallar community. I have heard that back in my grandfather's father's time, our community was 'number one' in the forest, and he would not allow any outsider to touch the water from our well and defile it. Such was the importance given to cleanliness in those days. Pappammayi's son Pazhanimala annan would often say that our clan was certainly not that which was mentioned in the Government documents. To put it accurately, our people belonged to the Malavedar clan. I think it could be true. Childhood memories of my grandfather leading men into the forest to collect honey from the bees now seem like a dream. Moreover, the bow and arrow were the first things that we would take out during special occasions.

Annan would often joke, "We would get nothing from the Government if we revealed our true clan name. The Government fellows would then say, 'You people belong to a clan that is above every other one. So what on earth can we give you?'"

I feel sad for Pazhanimala annan. His life was ridden with hardships. God did not will that he enjoy a happy married life with his wife Valli. Valli was always in pain. She had a hole in her heart. She bore him three children. All the three died. Eaten by pain bit by bit, she decided to end her life by jumping into the canal. Pazhanimala annan would sorrowfully tell us these stories from his life. He told us that he was trying to lessen the burden of his heart by pouring out his sorrow.

In the early days of our settling here, we adivasi people did not even have a proper graveyard to bury the dead. If someone died, we would carry the body for burial to the Gounder's forest lands in Tamil Nadu. Sometimes after crossing the Kerala border to reach the burial grounds in the forest, we were told off by the Gounders who came at us with sticks saying, "Why did you come here? You must not dump the corpse here. We will beat you up black and blue!"

I have heard the story of such a death. When Nakel's brother-in-law, Kannan, died of snakebite, they carried him as usual to the burial place in the same forest. On reaching there, they discovered that the Gounders had cultivated rice and millets on that ground in abundance. What could be done? Deciding to face the issue head-on, they left the corpse right there and returned home. When they were returning, the Gounders raised a hue and cry. Our people did not back off either. Finally they buried Kannan in the same place.

The Gounders threatened that they would break our legs if we went there again. After all how could we blame them? As far as they were concerned we were Malayali people.

Somehow God was with us. Before the next death happened, the collector arranged for a new burial ground in Nellimedu. What would we have done with our dead if this had not happened? Would we not have been reduced to the pitiable condition of burying our dead inside our houses?

A severe struggle was going on in Pazhanimala annan's heart. All sorts of people would ask him about the adivasis. The man would get furious and retort that such people are responsible for making the adivasis self-willed weaklings. When annan began speaking in this vein, he would go on and on. Personal stories would get mixed up with stories of the society. Poor annan, he was all alone in the world without son or daughter. He would eat whatever old ammayi was able to cook.

I have heard annan tell the story of cultivating red gram in the forest. He would ask, "Do you want to hear the story of how everyone cheated an adivasi?" Annan had leased a stretch of forest from Mathavan Moothar of Kannimari. Moothar demanded fifteen rupees as lease money. The mediator fixed it at thirty sacks of gram. It was a time when a bag of gram fetched six or seven rupees. However, that year the rains betrayed annan. The grams were infested with worms and became useless. He did not get even ten full bags of gram. It ended up in a court case. In the meantime, a few friends from his place helped him. But it was of no use. Annan lost the land. What can one do if cheated by both God and man? How many times must annan have walked up and down to pursue the court case! Finally, he was left with no money, no forest and no work.

It is a really sad situation. We who were known as the kings of the forest have now been brought low. We, who, as annan says, are of a superior rank. I wonder what refuge can be there for us who belong to such a category. None whatsoever. The misfortune of begging others for work as a supplicant with bent legs! The agony of waiting in long queues with pots for drinking water even during the monsoons! We are paying for our sins to that extent!

FIVE

The Troubles Begin

There are about twenty adivasi Colonies in and around Perumatty Panchayat and the neighbouring areas. All the inhabitants are migrants like us. These Colonies had names like Madhavan Nair Colony, Plachimada, Thottichipathy, Rajeev Nagaram, Kochikadu, Ottan Challa and Navanthodu – to name a few. Our Colony was named Vijayanagar when Vijayettan, son of Kathirvelu *muthalali,* became the Ward Member. Velur was named after Kathirvelu muthalali.

As I said earlier, when the Company came I did not feel that there was anything seriously wrong at first. The Anganwadi issue happened much later. When the drinking water started tasting increasingly bitter, we were all convinced about one thing. The water that came out of the Company was dirty and black. Since they used it to water the plants, we suspected that the dirty water had seeped into our wells as well. There were five or six Colonies located around the Company. Our Colony, Plachimada, Madhavan Nair Colony, Velur, Thottichipathy and Rajeev Nagaram were all close to the Company.

By and by the news about the water spread to all the Colonies. The water started turning worse. We could not use it to drink or cook. If we had a bath, our hair would turn sticky. If we used it to clean the vessels, our fingers would burn and itch. The moment we ate food, we felt the need to defecate. After that we would feel tired and drowsy. Our eyelids would become swollen.

At first, we did not understand the reason for all this. We went to hospitals in Nellimedu, Nanniodu, Chittur and Palakkad. Even the doctors in those hospitals could not tell

IMAGE 2: Mayilamma beside her unusable well in Vijayanagar Colony.

Source: Courtesy, Madhuraj, Senior Chief Photographer, *Mathrubhumi*.

what the matter was. They gave us tablets and syrups. We would take them. That was all. However, our ailments did not lessen. Gradually people started openly voicing their suspicions about the dirty water getting into our wells. Even then none of us knew what to do next.

But how long could we hide our suffering? So all of us came to a decision and went to meet Ward Member Varadettan. He said, "We will bring Jalanidhi water from Nellimedu." Was it our destiny to buy water with money? We did not agree to that. Since the time the Colony was built, there has been a Panchayat well. There was water, as though stored in a pot, in our courtyard wells too. Like household vessels brimming with water, the well in our courtyard was always full. Ignoring all this, what madness would make people think of buying water?

We were worried about what to do. Then it occurred to us that a licence was needed to run a big company, wasn't it? Getting a licence was not possible without the permission of the Panchayat. In that case we thought it would be enough if we explained our troubles to the Panchayat people. All of us got together and met the Panchayat President. The President promised us that the Colony would get water through pipes in a year's time. Krishnan Kutty, MLA, also said, "I will take care of it!" We came back trusting his words.

Meanwhile, the Company offered to supply us with water. We said no to them. These benevolent lords who had snatched away our water were now offering to bring us water from elsewhere! We were determined not to give in.

But we needed drinking water, didn't we? So we would walk two to two and a half kilometres every day to Kochikkadu and bring water. We were not able to go for work on the day we went to fetch water. The day we went to work, there was no water at home. There was no limit to our suffering.

Meanwhile, matters began to worsen. Added to the trouble with dirty water was the problem of two 'colour wastes' from the Company, one white and the other black. Both stank like rotting corpses. We were not able to swallow our rice. We felt nauseous. The Company passed it off as good fertiliser and asked us to use it in our fields.

During summer that year, the wells of all the farmers in the neighbourhood went dry. Water from the bore pipe which used to flow for two hours now stopped after half an hour. I wondered if what had happened in the Soya company was also happening here. Whatever it was, the farmers joined us whether in groups or singly.

It was in the middle of all this that Vilayodi Venugopalettan came to Plachimada. He was with the adivasis in Attapadi for many years. He came after Palana's son, Velur Swaminathan, told him about the state of affairs here. He was after all from our place. Things came to a head after that. People from all the Colonies decided to oppose the Company. In addition to this, we decided to talk about our problem to the Government and the political parties. We also formed a protest committee for this purpose. In the meantime, two years slipped past accompanied by hardships and suffering.

SIX

Childhood Memories

By the time the protest started, one and a half years had already passed since we started going to Kochikkadu to fetch water. Water was needed for the Anganwadi as much as it was needed for our homes. We had to think of the ayah and the lady teacher who took care of our children. Why did these people, who came from outside, have to share our sufferings and hardships? Surely it was not their fate to fetch and carry water. They would get their wages no matter if they prepared the rice gruel or not. In the early days we gave them water in return for money. Later it occurred to us that the salary they draw is as carefully measured and counted as deep fried *appams.* If they use it to buy water what will they do for their food and other livelihood needs? After that each household started taking turns to supply them water free of cost.

Now for the last two or three years, the Panchayat arranges for tankers to distribute water. Who knows about the quality of the water or where it is from? The man in the khaki pants who pumped water said that none of us would drink it if we were told where it was from. According to him, the water was collected from somewhere below a crematorium near the Chittur river. What could we do? We were helpless. Whatever the water's source, it was being offered to us for free, like a charity. We had no option but to drink it.

Newspapers such as the *Mathrubhumi* and *Madhyamam* are circulated in the *pandal*. We heard people read out from these papers that the rainfall was abundant in all places. Three or four months ago the members of the People's Society built us a tank to store rainwater. If it fills up, we will have some relief. Till then we have to depend on the tanker water.

I have to specially mention something here. Although we struggled for water, we did not close down the Anganwadi for a single day. It was the only place for our children to go to. They would get rice gruel and *uppuma* to eat in the afternoon. Polio drops and other vaccination shots were also distributed so that the children would not fall sick. But all said and done, our children are not in good health.

Occasionally I would go and spend time with the Anganwadi children. I would watch them sing and play. Rohini teacher would sing beautiful songs to them. One day I listened to Sundaran's son Manikandan singing a song from the pamphlet distributed in the pandal:

Perched on the top of a mango tree,
A Plachimada bird chirped:
"My throat is parched, dear people!
Your Coca-Cola surely cannot wet my parched throat!
O man from the alien shore,
I am not used to it.
My nest is here, so is my family, my land and its people.
After devouring the rice that quells our hunger,
After sucking dry the water from the Earth's womb
O man from the alien shore!
You and your lackies will leave with your bottles!"

Whenever I look at those children, I am reminded of my days spent in Muthalamada in Attayampathy till the age of fourteen when I got married. Fortunately these children are not subjected to our fate of wandering around aimlessly without any education whatsoever.

I remember going to a school as a child in Attayampathy. That school near Kuttetan's field remains the same even today. I think the school was started around the time when I went to study. Nowadays many of our people's children go to that school to study. I have not had much schooling, only a few months in class one.

There were six or seven teachers in the school. I am not able to recall all their names now. One Velappan *mash* used to teach us. He was tall and fair. Mash used to tell us stories and sing songs. In those days they did not teach us Tamil. They taught us only Malayalam. I have listened to the senior students reciting A-B-C-D in English in a singsong manner.

They would not allow the Eravallar children to study much. I remember Velappan mash and Krishnan Kutty mash coming home one day. They had come to request my parents to send us to school. I was happy to think that I could go to school. Getting permission from *ayyan* was a huge hassle. Same with my mother too. The muthalalis would get angry if the word 'school' was mentioned. They did not like it if we, the labourers' children, wanted to get educated. If we went to school, there would be a shortage of hands at work. Our muthalali tried to prevent us from going to school. However, my brother Vellaiyan and I were adamant. At last, we got permission. Only Muthamma, Koli and I—the women from our community who went to school in those days—are around today. Velappan mash is also very much alive. He must be around seventy-five. He is the owner of the school. Krishnan Kutty mash is no more.

I liked going to school very much. Three of us girls, Muthamma, Koli and I, and the boys, Ayyappan, Kaliappan and Arumugan, went to school together. We would play all the way to school. The boys would play with marbles. They would pluck castor seeds and burst them open. The road was studded with castor plants which were as tall as men. We were not worried about the thorns or the sticky goo. We would pluck the dried castor seeds and make a thali and play at getting married.

I do not remember having gone to school for one whole year. Everything ended before that. The women in the huts would bear children every year. The job of the older children was to take care of the babies. If the mothers stayed back at home to look after the kids, who would feed the family? Only if the mother went out to earn money would the family not suffer for food that day. So it did not matter even if one loved to go to school. When a baby girl was born after me, my ayyan said: "Mayila, you will have to take care of the baby. Let go of school and studies. Anyway why do girls need to study?" I tried telling him about my desire to study. I liked the trip to school, playing games and cracking jokes with my friends all along. But it did not turn out in my favour. My education came to an absolute halt.

Meanwhile, the muthalali's manager came home to say that the cows needed to be taken out for grazing. This was something that would fetch money. Ayyan and amma convinced me somehow and sent me for grazing cattle and cutting grass. On the first day of grass cutting, I went along with my amma. I did not even know how to hold a sickle. Boils erupted on my hand. When I recount this, something else comes to mind. When Sarasa was working in the groundnut field, something pricked her fingers. Boils appeared on two fingers, which rotted and fell off. This is how things happened as far as we are concerned. I feel all this is because of the lack of education and awareness. Our grandfathers, great-grandfathers and grandmothers knew the names of a lot of medicinal herbs. Nowadays our people do not have the knowledge which our ancestors possessed. At the same time, we are also not familiar with new medicines and methods of healing. No money either. What then? So we continue to pass our days like this in a state of living death!

Sometimes I feel angry with my parents. They did not think that their children should study the alphabet and get educated so that they would have a better future. We are facing problems now because of that. After dropping out, I next saw a school only when my children went to one. Our parents did not allow us to play as much as we wanted. When we went to work there was no time to play. Cutting the grass itself was hard work. You should see the face of the muthalali's overseer if, at the end of the day, the pile of cut grass weighed less. On such days, he would hold back some money from our meagre wages of four *annas.* Even if we cut grass till dusk, we would get only four annas. Amma would not allow us to buy even a candy from that money. I did not give my first wage to amma. I very badly wanted to have a tattoo done on my arm.

I used that money to get myself a tattoo of the temple pond in Mattupatti where we celebrate *Pongal.* The Dalit Thottichi women did the tattooing job. They would use some kind of a thorn to do it. While on the job they would sing a song. I have seen them tattooing *porattu* motifs and singing this song at a porattu performance. There are many humorous moments in a porattu dance. The questioner would ask the actor various questions. I would almost die of laughter hearing his hilarious replies. The porattu dance was usually performed at night. If my ayyan was in the right mind, he would let me go. However, I had to be accompanied by elders. Koli's parents would also come.

Similarly, the Ariyamala dance would be performed sometimes. Ariyamala's story would make us sad. For the next few days we would be occupied in the game of enacting it. We would put on a crown made from the leaves of the jackfruit tree and held together with the dried sticks of coconut leaves. Ayyappan was the king. Muthamma and Koli were the snake charmers. I was Ariyamala. Some of our games resembled our daily chores. Pounding grain, making rice and curry, and so on. We also played the game of grazing goats. The children used to hold their waists and walk bending their bodies, all the while bleating like goats. On hearing the goats' cry, the 'tiger' would emerge from the forest. We would then pretend that we were chasing the tiger away.

We would play these games when we went to the forest to graze the cattle. Girls were not allowed to go alone to take a dip in the lake. Ayyan would tell me to scoop water in a vessel and have a bath. So I did not even know how to swim. Amma told me to hide if some outsider appeared. However, she would never say no if we wanted to go to the forest. This was because the forest was like a mother to her.

We did not have proper clothes to wear. At the most we would drape a towel or a piece of our mothers' torn sarees around our bodies. I remember that when I became a big girl, ayyan got me a *chungudi* skirt, the colour of muskmelon. I also received a similar coloured cloth to wrap around my upper body. I do not remember wearing a blouse even at the time of my sister's marriage.

I remember the names of only a few of the children who used to come with me to graze the cattle. Maruthan, Kaliappan, Vellain and Natchimuthu were the older boys who used to come along with me. Koli comes to my mind more often than the others. She accompanied me like my own blood relative. For anything and everything, Koli and Mayila were always together. Whenever I remember her face, I feel a tug at my heart. The poor girl died of jaundice. I remember that day very well. It was the monsoon season when the rains were abundant. Since I could not go out to play, I did not know about Koli's illness. Or did my parents hide it from me because they thought that I would catch the disease? I learnt one day that Koli was no more. I could not believe it. I ran to Koli's house, crying all the way. Koli lay stretched on the floor, draped in a piece of saree, the air thick with the fragrance of incense sticks and *sambrani* smoke. A broken coconut was kept near her head. Koli's mother was lamenting in a loud voice. In my memory, this was the first death that I had ever seen. Koli was their only daughter. I now wonder how they bore their loss. Muthamma's marriage happened after mine. Married women of our community do not usually go to their place of birth. I, therefore, was not able to attend Muthamma's marriage. I do not even know where she lives now.

This is the lot of our womenfolk. Take, for instance, our house of birth. After getting married, ties with our parental home were of no use. The house into which we married became our home. A girl's parents would wash their hands of her after marriage. Whether her life then turned out to be good or bad depended on her husband's people. It was fine if the house into which the girl married was good; if not, how would her life be? Fortunately, my situation did not turn out to be like that. But God did not wish that I spend a long time with my husband. That is why He called my husband back very early.

SEVEN

Changing Times

I loved going to the forest to graze the cattle just as I loved going to school. In the forest I could wander around and play to my heart's desire. The muthalali or his overseer would not be there to roll their eyes at me. In the morning amma would prepare something and leave it on the stove before going away to work. There would be ragi *kali* or *chama* rice or just old leftover rice. Sometimes there would be nothing. I would gulp down whatever was available and go out to graze the cattle. All of us children would go in a group. We would not go deep into the forest. We used to come across deer, rabbits and peacocks in the outer parts of the forest where shrubs and small trees grew. During the night elephants and boars would enter the fields. Once, sitting on the high perch with my grandfather, I cried out loud on seeing an elephant walking into the field. The elephant was driven away by hurling lit torches and bursting fire crackers.

We would remain in the forest until dusk. Two or three of us would get together and graze the cattle. Others would search for crabs in every nook and cranny. Catching crabs is an interesting art. When we put our hands into their holes, the crabs would pinch us. After getting two or three pinches, we would grab them in a single smart lunge. Once we caught them, we would pull off their claws and keep them in water. Then we would look for fish to catch in the lakes and streams. There would be all kinds of fish like *paral, chodiyan* and *moyyu*. The sting of the moyyu's bone could leave you in great pain. Our stomachs would tell us when it was noon. Then we would tie up the cattle at some place, build a fire, roast the fish, crabs and the dug up tubers, and eat them. After that we had to run behind the cattle till dusk. In the middle of all this, we also had to pluck *rakkiri* from the forest. We call spinach 'rakkiri'. All kinds of rakkiri could be found in the forest—*kummitukeera, ponnangani keera, chukrumani keera, koyya keera* and many more. At night, back home we usually made a curry with spinach to go with the ragikali. Sometimes we would also wrap up in a leaf the crabs whose claws we had removed and take them them back home.

My amma would prepare an excellent crab curry. She would grind coriander seeds, pepper, cumin seeds and white garlic, and add tamarind pulp, and when the whole thing came to a fine boil, she would add the crab pieces and cook them. The smell would make my mouth water. Crabs can be used to clear the mucus from the chest. Pound the meat from the middle part of the crab and mix it with dessicated coconut milk. Boil the mixture after adding to it palm jaggery, pepper, cumin seeds and oregano seeds. Have a glass of this and take a nap in a place protected from the wind. Take a bath after the nap and have a meal of rice and pepper extract. There will be no question of mucus accumulating in your chest. These days in the towns sea crabs are being sold in the market. But they are of no great use. The small country crabs that you find in the field pits are the ones that are tasty and nutritious. Back then, poisonous fertilisers or pesticides were not used in the fields. Cow dung, decayed leaves and ash were the only fertilisers. Crabs in the fields these days must have become 'poison crabs' as they feed on chemicals! That is the reason they do not taste as good as they did once.

When we were children, my parents would take us to watch a *cilima* once in a while. The tickets cost an anna per head. The theatre was located in Kambarathu Challa. The first film that I watched was MGR's *Adimai Penn*. I remember that MGR's mother was a slave in that film. I have watched many films of MGR and Sivaji [Ganesan]. *Nadodi Mannan, Sivantha Mann* were the films that ran in those days. I watched

IMAGE 3: Mayilamma on a mud path flanked by the verdure of her village.

Source: Courtesy, *Mathrubhumi* archives.

two films with my husband after marriage, *Pettrathan Pillaiya* and *Kulanthaiyum Deivamum.* This generation likes actors like Rajini, Mohanlal and Mammootty.

Why talk about cilima now? We need to think only about when we are going to leave this world. Our days are all over. The coming days belong to our children. We need to think about how they are going to survive here. If we do that, there will be no time or money left to go and watch a cilima.

EIGHT

'This is Our Problem'

Today there are not too many people in the protest pandal. Most of the men have gone to work. Among the rest many have fever. I too had a headache from the morning. It felt as though the insides of my eyes were swollen. Muthuchamy's wife, Vasanthi, was going to hospital. I asked her to get me some medicine. I did not feel like going to the doctor I usually go to. Sarasal told me that she had seen him entering the Company two days ago. Somehow I get suspicious of anybody who goes to the Company.

Sarasal said that the Company people were distributing free medicine in the hospital in Palakkad. I heard from Lohia Vedi's man, Janardhanan Namboodiri Sir, that the Company was planning to set up a hospital and an English medium school. Who knows whether this was true or not? Whether it was for free or not, we, the Colony people, do not want anything from the Company. No medicines, tablets, books, clothes—none of these.

My granddaughter Sujitha is rocking herself in the cloth *thottil* hung in the pandal. She is the daughter of my youngest son, Supramani. His wife Rajamma has not been keeping well at all. Despite that, she has also been sitting in the pandal since morning. Palana's girl, Bhagyam, is preoccupied in removing the leaves from the drumstick stalks. Her little son Aneesh would run out on the road the moment we took our eyes off him. Two people were needed to keep a constant eye on the children coming to the pandal. The children were given only bread in the morning. Sarasal is preparing gruel. The rice donated by the Solidarity people was almost finished. The

IMAGE 4: Protest in front of the Coca-Cola plant at Plachimada.

Source: Courtesy, *Mathrubhumi* archives.

phone account with Muraliettan ran to a huge sum since we had made a lot of phone calls from his booth. Sometimes I wonder if I should phone anybody at all. It is hard enough to earn money even for our daily food.

The months of *Mithunam* and *Karkatakam* rolled in, but there was hardly enough rain. Thangamani from Plachimada Colony who had come to the protest pandal said, "If it continues like this, we will not even get the tanker water, Mayilamma!"

Thangamani is originally from Pattikulam; her husband is a Christian. They had two daughters. One was run over by a vehicle last year. The other one ran away with a Mappila boy. Now the old man and the old woman are all alone. Poor Thangamani. She appears older than she really is. There are about three hundred houses in Plachimada Colony. The houses with wells are very few in number. In those days the women from Plachimada Colony used to come to our Colony to draw water. They would discuss the goings-on in the Colony while filling water at the well. Thangamani was the leader of her companions. By the time a pot of water travelled from Vijayanagar to Plachimada, Thangamani would have exchanged a great deal of gossip.

The members of seven or eight households in Plachimada Colony go to work in the Company. They will not come to the pandal. They would get together and gossip about us. They showed their true colours when I asked them whether money alone was sufficient in place of fresh air, water and soil. If they are to be believed, no one had as many faults and blemishes as the people sitting in the pandal.

Sarasa would say, "They think they are very straightforward. They can say that because their men travel four or five kilometres every day to fetch water. Only if they do it alone will they understand the difficulty of it. Let us see what they do when the Company shuts down after drinking all our water."

"Why are the old women going to school?"

I opened my eyes on hearing Chembagam ask somebody this. The headache has not left me. Vasanthi was nowhere to be seen. Kaliappan's daughter, Kanniamma, and Kalichami's daughter, Nayaka, had gone to school to collect the books that were distributed free of cost. The faces of the children looked dull. I felt that the fever would spread. When I had gone to the Anganwadi in the morning, I noticed that there were very few children.

I remember that the Anganwadi was started sixteen years ago. The Government had approved of starting an Anganwadi here because there was no water shortage. How many people's feet we had to fall at in order to get it started! Helper Chella was telling us even yesterday that the first person to give a donation was our Minister *Mami*. Though nobody calls me that to my face, someone has given me the nickname, 'Minister Mami.' Whether in jest or in earnest I don't know.

Venuettan has taken a lot of trouble for us. His organisation works for the welfare of the people of Kerala. Now he is running around for our cause. He has stood by us for everything. When he first suggested that we should stage a protest, everyone including me was doubtful. Would we win? What would we do if there was no work? Why say more, even on the very day we began the protest, a few of them kept away. It was he who brought everyone together and explained the situation. Shaji would also pay a visit time and again.

Our people should take interest, shouldn't they? We must think of this as our problem. The Government has set up two centres for the adivasis here. One for the crafts and the other for tailoring. Venuvettan would tell us that we need to make proper use of what the Government gives us. Otherwise, he would warn, we would lose even the little we have. I share all this with as many people as I can reach out to. But at the end of the day, they too need to believe that all will turn out well.

NINE

Fertile Land, Rituals and Beliefs

In those days even if the rains failed, we never suffered for want of water. The water from the Aliyar dam would fill the Kambalathara lake. From there the water would flow into the Venkalakkayam dam and the Moolathara canal. The water was abundant up to places like Chittur and Peruvambu. The fields were like swamps, rich in water. The rice plant would grow twice a year. If you stood in the field, your feet would sink in the slush. Men and women were not allowed to work in the same place since women wore clothes barely enough to cover themselves and had to sit on the slushy ground with their legs stretched out in order to plant the seedlings. The earth was so fertile in those days.

When the forest was cleared, rice was grown in the low plains while maize, cotton, horse gram and millets were planted on the high flatlands. Cultivation was done according to the seasons. There would be work around the year. What was given as wages was not money but a share of the harvest. The wage depended on the year's produce. So what if it was back-breaking work? One could take heart that wages would be given without fail in the evening. One did not have to worry whether there would be work the next day. Although the forests had gone, the adivasi people did not suffer. There were plenty of jobs which they were good at.

Ragi was harvested in the month of *Aadi*. It was the time when the rains would pour. A share of the sheaves was our wages for harvesting ragi. They would arrange them in four or five heaps. Similar to how vegetables are piled up in the bazaar. One part out of five went to the labourers. The rest went to owners of the forest. By the time the workers collected their share and got home, it would be dusk. They would thresh the grainstalks by stamping on them, then sieve the grains in a *muram*, heat them and finally pound them using a grinding stone and make flour. Then they would pour the flour into a pot of boiling water and stir it with a ladle. The ragikali would come out as a thick lump. Using a coconut shell as a ladle, they would serve balls of kali to everyone. The curry would be simply a mixture made of rakkiri, onion and chillies grown in the forest. In those days the bowls for eating from were made by the potter. Everybody used to eat from them.

The *chama* grain sheaths would be bundled and threshed by bulls; the grains would then be sieved, roasted and pounded to make rice. Bottle gourd leaves were added to the chama grains before they were roasted. Chama rice was eaten with spinach curry. Corn was washed and pounded. The grains of corn were shiny. When cooked, the rice would gleam like pearls. Stewed horse gram was the side dish for corn rice. It was only during the horse gram harvest that we were adequately compensated for our labour. We would pluck ripe horse gram pods from the vine of the plant and bring them home. When we threshed them, we easily got a yield of one to one-and-a-half *para* of horse gram. If we dried the grain and stored it, it would last for a whole year without being spoilt by cockroaches or worms. If we had corn rice and stewed horse gram once a day, we could easily go without any other food for the rest of the day.

The people who went to Tamil Nadu to work in the Gounders' fields learnt a lot of songs from them. In those days I used to sing those songs while working. It helped everyone forget their hunger and fatigue from hard work. Velur Swaminathan's mother, Palana, and Selvi's aunt, Sarasal, were the lead singers. Sarasal's lullabies could put even grownups to sleep:

Close your eyes and go to sleep,
O my flower-like son!
Go to sleep.
Why are you crying?
Who beat you?

Are you sobbing
because mother is not to be found?
There is nobody to fondle you,
because mother is not to be found.
The apple of my eye,
go to sleep!
O my forest beetle,
go to sleep!
This is a gift from your maternal uncle,
who spliced the illupa tree into half
and hung swings on either side;
and applied collyrium with a leaf and a straw
to your unsleeping eye.

Children these days do not care about those songs. They are happy with songs that come out of radio boxes.

While planting the seedlings, Palana would sing at length. The rest of them would join in a chorus:

In the four-cornered field
Thillelelalelo!
Plant the seedlings my sisters,
Thillelelalelo!
The seedling planted by the short girl
Thillelelalelo!
is shaking all over
Thillelelalelo!
Keep planting over there,
Thillelelalelo!

There is another song:

Here he comes, here he comes!
Here comes the pannadi!
Holding a green umbrella,
Here he comes to see the crops!
Holding a blue umbrella,
Here he comes to see the field!

Nowadays, I am not able to recall the words of those songs very well. We would collect honey from the forest, mix it with millet flour and eat it. While we kneaded the dough, we would sing a song. The song tells a story. Velavar who chanced upon Valli shooing away the birds in the millet field fell in love with her and approached her in the guise of an old man. Valli took pity on the old man and kneaded millet flour with honey and gave it to him. The old man held her tight in an embrace. Valli cried in fear and called out to her brothers. Before they could come Velavar transformed himself into a *venga* tree. In the end when Vinayaka came in the form of an elephant and frightened Valli, she embraced Velavar. That is how they got married.

Lord Subrahmanya is our clan deity. We will never cut a venga tree. Since Velavar rides on a peacock, we never kill peacocks either. Like this, every clan has its own deity. Velavar is the deity for us who belong to the Raja Kulam. Madurai Veeran is the deity for people of the Sembuthan clan. For the Panna clan it is Karupparayan. These are some of the adivasi gods.

The most important festival we celebrate is Pongal. It falls in the *Makara* month and is celebrated for three whole days. On the first day of the *Margazhi* month, we make an idol of *Pillaiyar* out of cowdung, keep it in the courtyard and worship it. The girls sing songs and dance the *kummi* in a circle. On the first day of *Thai*, pongal is offered to Ganesan. The second day is *Pattipongal*. On that day the forest muthalalis come with their children and family to the fields. There are seven pongal pots. Pongal is cooked in all the seven pots, and offered to seven deities like Murugan, Karupparayan, Kaliatha, Mariatha and others. Afterwards a *teppakulam* is made with seven stones brought by seven virgins. They place pineapple leaves, *plachi* flowers, sugarcane and palmyra fronds inside and decorate it. They pour the water used to clean the pongal rice into the pots. On a round plate they place a ritually purified saree and *prasadam*, and feed the latter to the calves. Then they make a Pillaiyar out of wild turmeric root and worship it. They make festoons out of mango and *manathakkali* leaves for the bulls and later set them free. The bulls tear down the festoons and muddy the teppakulam water. The ritual ends with that. That day all the labourers have their meal at the muthalali's house.

The evening after the ritual was over the barber, the washerman and the cobbler would go from house to house beating the *tapatta.* The thirty-day-old cowdung Pillayar, placed on a plate along with offerings like gram, beaten rice, puffed rice and banana would be brought along. We would keep all of these in the village centre and pray. A meeting and a song would follow.

O Pillayare!
I brought you up
by binding my hungry mouth
and stomach.
O Pillayare!
Are you going to drift away
in the waters of the canal?
Sister Palmyra leaf
who wears a basket of screw pine flowers in her knotted hair
is calling,
O Pillayare!
Come out of hiding and come running.
He ran away and hid in the Ottapullar temple
because he didn't find a comb.
If you don't have a comb
I will give you a comb!
O Pillayare !
Come out of hiding and come running.

The story goes that since Vinayaka did not have a comb he went and hid among the Ottanmar people who are stone masons. This meeting is convened to sing songs and hail Vinayaka. We would keep singing and immerse the idol in water. This is how the Pongal festivities would end.

Those were the days! These days there are no rituals or festivals. Getting our daily meals on time itself has become quite an achievement. Also a demon has arrived which is sucking up all the water and destroying everything around. The rich muthalalis have bought up the remaining lands and converted them into coconut groves. What work do we have there now?

Previously, once a year we had to dig up and loosen the ground around the coconut trees, apply fertiliser and inspect the tree tops. If they buy a machine, they do not even need a person to water the trees! The owner had to just tap a switch. This is how we ended up without any work on most days. But now we have got a new job—squatting in the protest pandal! The youngsters who returned from work in the evening would join us in the pandal. We would get together and spend time singing songs and discussing our hardships. It was then that fathers and mothers would narrate the stories of their childhood and its flavours.

TEN

Family Ties and Hard-working Women

My ayyan and amma lived in Aattayampathy in Muthalamada Panchayat. My ayyan's name is Raman and my amma's, Kurumanda. My ayyan's father was called Komaran, his mother's name was Kanniamma. They had three children, including one daughter. However, we lost touch with her when she was given away in marriage to someone from Kallavaram in Tamil Nadu. My ayyan was the eldest son of my grandparents. I remember my grandfather very well. He was an impressive looking man. As I said, we belonged to a clan called Raja Kulam. My husband Marimuthu belonged to the Chembuthan Kulam. The children came under the father's clan. People would not marry within the same clan since that would be just like a marriage between a brother and a sister. People followed these rules rigorously in those days. I have heard that Pappammayi's elder sister's husband used to select brides by strictly observing clan rules. Nowadays nobody bothers about all that. My second son Thangavelu married a girl called Mini from Koduvayur in Kakkoor. His horoscope indicated that he would marry a girl from Kerala. The man who married my daughter Deivana was my uncle's son Supramani. According to the Tamil custom he was my daughter's *moraimaman*. My elder son Murugaraj married my elder brother's daughter Lechumi. Supramani, my youngest son, was the only one who followed the clan rules for marriage. Rajamma from Thothichipathy is his wife.

My amma's father's name was Kannan and her mother's, Kanniamma. They were also from Muthalamada Panchayat. My father and grandfather had their own lands. In the beginning they lived off the land by working on it. It was during their old age that they leased the lands to the Gounders and the Mappilas. In those days, the patta titles were engraved on copper. I remember playing with it as a little girl. Seeing me doing this, my grandfather took it away from me and gave it to the muthalali for safekeeping. I do not think we got it back after that. By the time my ayyan married amma and brought her home, my grandfather had lost all his lands. So my parents had to make their living by working on someone else's lands. Later we lost our house too and by the time I got married, we were living in a rented house. In those days the muthalalis were sympathetic to our plight. How could they not be so? They needed people to work. They would get food only if the adivasis cleared the forest, created agricultural land and laboured on it. They would give us a meagre sum of five or ten rupees for our work in addition to food. We ignorant fools took them to be kind and generous! What did we know except toiling hard? Our people lacked the intelligence or common sense to realise that they were being duped. All that the menfolk cared about was the ten or fifteen rupees that they got as wages which came in handy at the toddy shop. It is really a pity! If only they had a little more brain, we would not have suffered the way we did.

In those days, 'work' meant back-breaking labour. We barely had time to do our daily chores. We had to get up at five in the morning. One had to attend to more than one job at a time. The fields would always be filled with water. On one side the ripened grain that had to be harvested would wait for us, on the other, the tilled field that had to be seeded. The workers had to finish all these jobs before dusk in order to get their daily wages. My ayyan and amma were given one measure of paddy as wages for every twenty sheaves that they had harvested. It would get really late when we went to sleep since the paddy had to be pounded, roasted and cooked as a meal for the family. We did not have kerosene to light the lamps. We would dry castor oil seeds in the sun, string them on broom sticks and set them on fire. All the work done at night in our house was by this light. We would have time only for a short sleep. If there was rice in the house, we had to wake up early. We had to cook our midday meal before leaving. If there was nothing to eat, we would set off to work just like that.

At six in the morning we would go to our portion of the field, bind the grain stalks that we had cut, place them on the ridge and eat leftover rice from the previous day's cooking. By the time we finished doing so, the men would have finished ploughing the land. We would then sow the seeds or plant the seedlings. At noon we would take the bound rice sheaves to the floor, thresh, winnow and clean them and later report on the measure of the yield. After collecting our wages, we would get back home, fetch water and prepare our meal. It would be quite a while before we went to sleep.

When compared to those days, women today do not have to work so hard. In the past, three or four women would stand and pound the grains using a mortar and pestle to make rice. These days there is a machine for doing all this. To cut grain, to grind grain—for everything. The tractor does the ploughman's job. So what happened was that there were no paddy jobs for us any more. However, there was also a positive change. We wanted our children to get educated and not roam around aimlessly. We wanted their futures to be moulded properly so that they would walk tall like the rest of society. So, the good thing as far as the children are concerned is that their mothers always keep an eye on them. The menfolk on the other hand seem to have an easy time. After the day's work, they may or may not choose to give money to their families. It is then left to us women to shoulder the burden. If work was available, we had to take it up and also look after the household. We also had to worry about what would happen to our children in the days to come. These considerations did not matter to the menfolk. They would shove a few notes into the hands of their mother or wife. This done, they would go after toddy, liquor, cilima...that was about all.

ELEVEN

Marriage and Early Widowhood

I attained puberty only three months before marriage. A girl who has come of age would be made to sit all alone by herself. Her uncles would build a hut thatched with green coconut leaves in which the girl would be made to stay for seven or fourteen days. Every day a different snack would be served. A person would be entrusted with the task of attending to the girl's needs. It was truly a period of comfort and rest. For the *seer varisai* ritual, people would bring the girl snacks. Even today my mouth waters when I think of the oily *oppittu* made from the ground paste of rice and dried red chillies. The girl would be a totally different person when the fourteen-day period got over. I was the youngest girl in the family. Eleven girls were born before me. But none of them survived. Now it is just me and my two elder brothers.

On the fifteenth day, the girl's female relatives would surround her, tie the ends of sarees, fashion a makeshift chariot and take her to the lake for a ritual bath. They would comb her hair, adorn her and bring her home to the accompaniment of drumbeats. By then her uncles would have burned down the ceremonial hut. They were entitled to receive a palmful of oil, a pot of hot water, a new *vetti* and a towel.

On that day the girl would be made to sit in a secluded portion of the house verandah that was plastered with cow dung. The next morning, all the community folk would be invited for a feast that was served in a pandal. The sisters-in-law and aunts would compete with one another to bring a rich array of seer varisai. It was customary for the aunts to escort the girl to the pandal and fill her lap with gifts. They would fill the upper end of the saree with fruits, beaten rice, betel leaves, areca nuts, flowers and vermilion before binding it into a knot. It was customary to place a bow and arrow before beginning these rituals.

He came asking for my hand in marriage three months after I attained puberty. When he came accompanied by his uncle, I was grazing the goat in the ragi field patch near the forest. Uncle asked me, "*Ammini*, where are your ayyan and amma?" I wondered who they were. I asked them to sit down and went about my chores. It was dusk by the time my parents returned. They had observed me at work all the while. So they liked me very much. Later the groom's mother, his brother and wife all got together and offered thirty-five rupees as bride price and asked for my hand in marriage. Rice and paddy were also given as part of the bride price. Our folk do not have to suffer if a daughter is born. The boy's people usually bear nearly three-fourths of the wedding expenses.

I also remember that when his brother's wife pointed me out to her little son and said, "This is your Chitti!" I got annoyed at being called that and beat her.

It was only after the engagement got over that another uncle from Ooty came over and said that I was going to be Marimuthu's second wife. His first wife and her child had both died during childbirth. On hearing this, all of us were upset. Ayyan was unhappy that they had cheated him. Everybody thought that the marriage would not take place. Later Marimuthu came to make peace with us. He said that he hid the details of his first marriage from us only because he liked me a lot. Later when we went to an astrologer and asked him to take a look at my horoscope, he told us that I was destined to be a second wife. If that was the case, everybody agreed that we could go ahead with the marriage.

I did not even know what marriage was all about. My ayyan told me that they were giving me away in marriage so that I could cook for Marimuthu. However, I was puzzled about who had cooked for the man all these years.

Our weddings did not have too many rituals. However, there were a few of those. On the day before the wedding, in the afternoon, the groom's people would bring ceremonial gifts of ground wild turmeric and spiked ginger, an *idangazhi* of rice, seven banana leaves, seven bundles of betel leaves and seven unripe bananas to the bride's house. Then the groom's family was served food. At the crack of dawn, the aunts and sisters-in-law would give the bride a bath. I do not know if this is a Tamil custom. The uncle would then make the bride place her foot on the *ammi,* point out the Arundhati star to her and put a ring on her toe. In the morning the groom's people would arrive bringing new clothes, *pottu* and flowers. Afterwards the groom would tie the thali around the bride's neck and take her home. My marriage was held in this manner. The marriage rituals were different during my mother's time. On the day of the wedding, the womenfolk from the groom's side would come over, adorn the bride, take her to the groom's house and conduct the marriage there. It was customary to carry the bow and arrow during all these comings and goings.

During the thali tying ceremony, the elders would publicly announce the marriage. They would loudly proclaim the names of the bride and groom and the clans from which they hailed. Before all this took place, they would sing a song in a chorus. It goes like this:

I ran North
Yes, I did.
There I saw a flowering tree
Yes, I did.
Wanted to pluck a flower from the tree
Yes, I did.
And stick it in my kondai.
At last I realised
Yes, I did.
That I did not like the flower.

The song would continue in this manner and at the end, the clan chief would declare that he was going to wear the flower plucked from the tree growing in the north. Then he would seek permission from the members of the community and sanction the marriage. Likewise, when the bride left for her groom's house after the marriage, the elders would crack jokes. This is what the girl's clan chief would say:

Our girl will carry rice and grain in her lap,
She will gather eatables in her lap,
To eat on her way to the mountain,
To eat on her way to fetch water,
To eat on her way to move her bowels.

What he meant to say was that the groom's people should take good care of a girl who likes to eat well all the time. I felt humiliated to hear this at that point of time.

In my case, the clan chief had an additional thing to say, "You married a young girl by hiding the truth. To compensate for that, this is what you'll have to do: for any ceremonies related to this girl, be it a childbirth or death, no one will come from our place. You should take care of all such expenses!"

Using this argument that the groom's people had cheated us, my ayyan, amma and the people of my village sent me on my way.

I came to Perumatty after this and began my married life, bearing children and raising a family. I had six children before I was twenty or twenty-one. In those days we lived in Velur. Three years after we moved to Vijayanagar, God called my husband back to Him.

Kalathuputhur is on the way from Perumatty to Attayampathy. Attayampathy comes under the Muthalamada Panchayat in Kerala. Perumatty is also in Kerala. But Kalathuputhur which comes in between is in Tamil Nadu. If you take the road from Nellimedu, Tamil Nadu will be on the left side and Kerala on the right. Ganapathipalayam is on the Tamil Nadu border.

My elder brother Vellaiyan and younger brother Nachimuthu lived in Kalathuputhur. Lechumi was Vellaiyanannan's daughter. After Deivana's marriage was over, it occurred to me that Murugan also needed a girl. So I went straight up to my elder brother and asked for his girl's hand in marriage. He consented. This is how Murugan married Lechumi. After the marriage, they did not stay in Perumatty.

According to Murugan, it is more comfortable to stay in Tamil Nadu than in Kerala. At present it is Amma's government there. I do not care about what people say about Jayalalithaa Amma, but I think she has done a lot for our people. She has given us houses, water, electricity, rice, clothes – everything. Once my husband suggested that we could stay with my brothers. We even got some land there. But he abandoned the plan later on, saying that it was a bother to have close relatives living nearby.

We went to Velur in Perumatty after getting married. Those were the days! My husband was about thirty at that time. I would feel frightened to look him in the eye. If he came near or called out to me, I would not go near him! I would hide and keep out of his way. When I saw him drinking toddy, my fear increased all the more. Although he had all these habits, I later realised that he was very fond of me. His first wife's name was also Mayilamma. He never called me by my full name because he was afraid of being reminded of her.

He liked to eat freshly caught fish. On days when there was no work, he would take his fishing rod and set out. He would also take the children along. There was a stream called Pappathivellam near Kalathuputhur. He would fish there. The three kids would frolic and play in the water till noon. He would catch fish, gather them on a stick and bring them home. If he visited the toddy shop on the way back, I could tell from the way he called me. I can still hear his voice ringing in my ears. In moments of great affection or after drinking toddy he would call me, "Da...*Kanna*... Mayila!"

He died when I was twenty-seven years old. He had been sick for three years. His chest was filled with phlegm. The doctor said that he had tuberculosis. We took him to hospitals in Chittur, Kozhijampara, Coimbatore, Oddanchatram and Palakkad. He breathed his last in a hospital in Palakkad. I can never forget the last moments of his life when he placed his head on my lap and looked at me with tear-filled eyes.

I rued my fate at the thought of bringing up four small children singlehandedly at that age. "Oh God! How is it possible?" I felt totally crushed. However, I spoke words of courage and comfort to my mother-in-law. "Don't think you have lost your son. Think that he is alive and continue staying with us. I will feed you."

But she did not stay with us. I remember very well what my mother-in-law told me that day. "Mayilu, you are not that old. You are a young girl! What will people say if you remain single raising these four children? Please marry someone. If you don't, you and these children will be orphaned."

Somehow I did not feel like it. At least, I still had the four children who were the fruit of my womb. How could another man or even four men give me what my own husband could not? Even if I got married, how would a man who is normally reluctant to take care of his own children take care of another man's children?

I had only one aim in my life. I wanted to bring up my children well. That was all.

Some people went to my ayyan and amma asking for my hand.

They replied, "Good that you asked us this question. If this had reached Mayila's ears, there would have been trouble!"

That is how this Mayilamma entered into life's battle at the age of twenty-seven.

TWELVE

A Dedicated Mother

In those days I looked at life with a tenacious eye. All my struggles and problems started when my man became bedridden. We spent quite a lot of money to buy medicines and consult doctors.

When I got married and entered the family as a young bride, I did not know a thing. I wept and kicked up a fuss because I feared that my relatives would leave after abandoning me in my husband's house. Therefore, my ayyan, amma and the people of my village had to wait till I fell asleep before returning to Attayampathy.

At the age of fifteen when I had no idea about pregnancy and childbirth, Murugaraj was already in my womb. I was quite scared then. It was the month of *Purattasi,* what we call *Kanni* in the Malayalam calendar. The season when the groundnuts were ready for picking. When at work, we would roast the nuts and eat them in the forest itself. I loved to scrape and prise open the ragi stalks and eat the grains. I panicked when I got labour pain. "Aiyayo! I ate too many groundnuts and millets and now my stomach is aching!" I cried aloud. When the pain increased, I thought that I was going to die. In those days, unlike today, there was no practice of going to the doctor if one missed one's monthly period. Nobody went to the hospital to deliver. I was not mature enough to understand the double meaning in the jokes and laughter of other women. On that day, my mother-in-law was not around. She had gone to Velur with my sister-in-law, Mutha. It was Pappamma, the Gounder woman in the next house, who came to my help. There was a woman named Ponnatha in the neighbouring Colony who practised medicine. She took a look at me and said, "Don't be afraid, girl! It will be over in ten minutes." I thought I would die in those ten minutes. However, my stomach pain did stop in ten minutes. That was how my son Murugaraj was born. We also called him Murugan.

Whenever she came to visit Pappammakka, Ponnatha would gently spank infant Murugan on his buttocks and say teasingly, "Mayila, do you see this boy who was born out of your stomach pain?" Poor lady, she was like the mother goddess. I slowly began to understand a lot of things. My other children are Deivana, Thangavelu, Supramani and Ponnan. I gave birth to one more son; but God did not give a long life to him and Ponnan. Ponnan died at the age of five after he caught a fever. His younger brother was stillborn.

I gave birth to Thangavelu where there was no adult around to help me. Three-year-old Murugan and two-year-old Deivana were with me. When I was walking up and down after the labour pain started, Murugan looked after Deivana and made sure that she did not come near me. He told his sister, "Ammini, amma is not feeling well. Don't go near her! A little one is going to drop out of amma's stomach!" I was telling this to Murugan's wife the other day and laughing about it for a long time.

In those days we were living in Velur. After that we moved to Vijayanagar Colony where we got a house in the *micha bhoomi* land.

When my husband lay ailing, barbed words were spoken by his brother's wife who came to visit. I still remember those words which singed my heart like fire.

"It is not enough if you give birth to a litter of children like a bitch. You have to worship a powerful God or give birth to intelligent children."

O God, why was I being criticised for things I was not even aware of? I felt wounded that those who should be standing by me were blaming me. This feeling changed into anger and determination. Her children were educated. The eldest one had studied up to the tenth standard. That is where her pride came from.

I took a decision. Even when my husband was alive, I would lie that he had married another woman so that my children would get admission to the hostel. Even in those days, Murugan was a mother's boy. He could not bear my suffering. So he stayed back. By that time, Deivana also started helping me out by doing small jobs. She wanted to study. Poor girl! She had to make way for her younger brothers to study. Thangavelu studied up to the tenth standard and Supramani up to the eighth.

I worked hard and earned money. After Deivana came of age, I celebrated her marriage with great pomp. My brother-in-law's wife who had criticised me also came to attend the wedding. I was able to make her say, "Mayila you are a clever one!" I think it was God who gave me the strength to achieve all this.

Deivana's marriage was the first to be held. I was eager to conduct it without missing even a ritual. But she gave me misery during that time. She told me that she was in love with her uncle, Supramani. In the end, everything happened according to her wish. They have a child now and are doing well.

I have raised my children and they are now well settled with families of their own. Now at the age of fifty-four when all my duties are over, I look back and wonder if I had prayed to a powerful God or given birth to intelligent children. It gave me satisfaction to think that I had not lived a 'bitch's life'. I was able to prove this to the people who had once found fault with me.

THIRTEEN

Protest: The First Year

We decided to begin the protest on 22 April 2002. I learnt it was a special day—Earth Day! For poor people like us, could there be a more appropriate day than this to fight for our soil, air and water?

On that day the people from the Company tried to create a rift among us. They promised jobs and water. Some of us fell for that bait. Later Venuettan and others spoke to everyone and made them understand. In spite of this some people went back to work. Such people are bound to be everywhere, I guess.

On the morning of the first day of the protest, a procession of cars carrying C. K. Janu and others came to Plachimada. It was Janu who inaugurated the protest; we put up a pandal and launched the protest. It was decided that all of those who could join the protest should sit in the pandal. No one gave much thought about how long the protest would last. During the discussions Vijayakumarettan had clearly told us that they would not close the Company in a jiffy and leave as we expected them to. One of the leaders told us a Christian story. The story of a small boy named David who defeated a giant called Goliath. Our fight with the Company was very similar to this story! They told us that in the story it was the boy who won the fight. We thought that like David, we would also win the battle even if it took a long time.

Janu told us a lot of things that day. We felt inspired when she told us about the protest in her place. We made up our minds that we would not give in just like that. Janu assured us the full support of the Gothra Maha Sabha. We were delighted to hear this. But, looking back, I feel hurt when I think

IMAGE 5: The protest pandal in front of the Coca-Cola plant at Plachimada.

Source: Courtesy, *Mathrubhumi* archives.

about Janu. The Muthanga incident took place shortly after we began our protest. The police arrested Janu and put her in jail. All of us felt as if one among us had been persecuted. So we went to Palakkad and staged a demonstration carrying lighted *ranthal* lamps. We even went to Thiruvananthapuram to meet Janu. We consoled her saying that we were with her. However, after being released from jail, Janu did not seem to care about us. The other day when the Mahila Sangham meeting was held in Palakkad, Janu had come along with Ajitha teacher. She also came to the protest pandal for a day. However, the intimacy that she showed us in the early days was now missing. I do not know if this was merely our assumption. But we were deeply hurt by this. I think that all of us who get together for a cause must be united; our strength lies in it.

The members of Ayyankali Pada were also with us for two months, offering all possible help and support. They even organised a big adivasi meeting. They left us after that and reappeared ten months later. By that time we had experienced a lot of hardships during the protest.

Prema teacher of Porattam alone would come very often. She would sit in the pandal and talk to us a lot. She would always eat a ladle of rice with us before leaving.

Many people used to visit when the protest was going on. They would all express their solidarity for our cause before leaving. Big people like Medha Patkar also came. So did a lot of writers like Sarah Joseph teacher, Sugathakumari teacher, Vasudevan Nair Sir and Azhikode Sir. The judge, Krishna Iyer Sir, had also come. Later, people from distant countries also started coming. They enquired about our problem in their language. The people who accompanied them made them understand what we said by translating our words. I cannot even pronounce the names of those people. We did not understand a word of the speeches they made in different languages. There would be some speech or other all the time. Everybody said the same thing. Listening to these speeches over and over again, I also learned to speak on stage. Even if this had not been the case, I believe that the words would have come naturally to me because my mind was overflowing with so many thoughts. Nowadays people take me to many places to speak and light the lamp during inaugural ceremonies of this and that.

Wherever I go, I have only one thing to say, "Our air, water and soil belong to us alone! We will always fight against those who try to destroy them."

Speaking in this vein day in and day out has made me forget my Tamil. I now found myself capable of switching to Malayalam when the occasion demanded it.

A few days after we started the protest, people began scoffing at us: "Fools! Sitting to protest without going to work! What can you achieve by fighting against such a big Company? You don't have even a spare set of clothes to wear or a small piece of soap to clean yourselves! Sitting down to protest? If your bellies went empty for four days, you would get up and leave!" The women who did the job of cleaning bottles in the Company would comment that we sat in the pandal because we were too lazy to work!

Somehow the protest reached its fiftieth day! On that day, Dr Nandakumar Sir came from Ernakulum to participate in the procession in Plachimada and also to give a talk. I saw with my own eyes a man among us telling the police that we must be beaten to pulp. That is exactly what the police almost did during the protest. We were accused of bringing in extremists. When the police started beating up Nandakumar Sir's driver, I tried to intervene and stop them, for which I was verbally abused by a policeman.

When the fifty-fifth day of the protest passed, we did something new. We collected the Company's fertiliser that was used in the field of the farmer, Sreedharettan, and spread it out at the entrance of the Company. We thought they should also get to know what a foul smell was like. There was a lot of violence that day. Ambikal's thali thread was cut and her clothes were torn. Many people were taken away to the police station.

One day we went on a procession to the Panchayat office. I do not remember the date. We even flung cow dung at the Panchayat office. All of us were so angry. We felt that all political parties were against us. They must have thought that supporting people like us, who had no education or awareness, was a waste of time. How can the poor adivasi people measure up to the level of the muthalali bosses in the Company? They wanted our votes. We all knew the price of a vote. Each and every leader would come up to us and ask for votes. We would believe their tall claims and end up voting for them. In the Panchayat the Janata Dal was the ruling party, while the MLA belonged to the Congress and the MP to the Marxist. We thought that all these parties would be with us during the protest. So why should we fear the Company's power? Water is needed at the time of both birth and death. They have snatched this precious water from our hands. We will fight with whoever supports the Company and opposes our protest.

Every household will fetch seven or eight votes. We are not prepared to donate those votes and sit at home like bobbleheads. Achuthettan asked us to vote for him. We did that. He promised us water in ninety days. The Panchayat President told us that it would take one year. Krishnadasettan, the Marxist party leader, told us that he would be with us whether we win or lose our fight. Are all these assurances enough? How long can we survive on the strength of these hollow words and promises?

We marched up to the MLA's house carrying brooms. Everyone was with us. I could not go that day. All this is what I heard from Ambikal. The MLA told them, "Going by your activities today, I don't think you are here to inform me about a wedding or a funeral. Why didn't you come to me first?"

What can we do if people in powerful positions tell us this? There is nothing else we can do but feel the pain.

Protests, public speeches, processions, rallies, humiliation—that is how a year passed. In the meanwhile, all sorts of people came and left. Some of them, I heard, had come to test the purity of water. They declared that the water was unfit for drinking. Likewise, the Company's fertiliser was tested in Thiruvananthapuram. I heard that the results proved that there was no 'fertiliser' in it! It became clear to me as the days went by that the Company brought ruin to the people of the place and nothing else.

FOURTEEN

The Protest: A Thousand Days

In the middle of all this hullabaloo, the Panchayat decided to go ahead with the job of laying a pipeline. They dug a huge well in Kambalathara and laid pipes from there via Kunchimenonpathy, Nellimedu, and Saralipathy to Meenakshipuram.

Water flowed through these pipes for two or three months. Then it stopped.

One day, nearly two months after the protest began, somebody erected a stage in front of the Company's entrance and began making speeches. When we listened carefully to these speeches, we came to know from these big people that we were not proper Malayali adivasis. They said that since we spoke Tamil, we belonged to Tamil Nadu! What can we say if they start speaking like this? Senseless idiots! If we belonged to Tamil Nadu, then what about half the population of Palakkad—the Iyers, the Chettiars, the Ravuthars and so on? Was it right to say that they were not Malayali people? How were we different? For ages the majority of the people here have spoken Tamil. Is it our crime that we were born in the borderlands?

On that day, they brought a lot of adivasi people from outside for the protest. The speakers insisted that these outsiders were the genuine adivasis, and not us.

Well, God's plans were different! We adivasis always recognise one another. When the public speeches got over, our adivasi friends came to the protest pandal. Their leader confessed that they did not know that they had been brought here for this purpose. It appeared that they belonged to the

Malasar community. These poor people had been told that there was a meeting at Palakkad, and that they would get food and wages if they attended it. They were on good terms with us. How can those people who wickedly set our own people against us talk of justice? As Narayanji told us during one of his visits, they might have hoped to achieve something by leaving us to fight among ourselves.

Moreover, after a hundred days of the protest, the Company people tried another trick. All the Company workers from places like Pollachi, Attayampathy, Muthalamada, Vandithavalam and Meenakshipuram comprising men, women and children were bundled off in thirty-five buses to Thiruvananthapuram. They were taken to voice their support for the Company for which they were given food and two hundred rupees each. This was revealed to me by a man who went on that trip. Ajayettan lives in Thiruvananthapuram. He is a lawyer. He has a large network of people there. It was only because of Ajayettan's timely intervention that the Company was not able to execute its evil plan. Finally when the secret was out, the Company tried to cover it up by saying that the adivasis had gone on a tour. But tourist buses are so expensive. How could the adivasi people afford to hire these buses? Everyone in our place came to know that the Company had paid for the transport of these people. What's more, I also heard that people who were promised two hundred rupees came back with nothing. Well, I could not say that they did not get anything. I heard that everyone got two bottles of Cola each!

Do you know the kind of pinpricks the Company people gave us to try and sabotage the protest? They dropped poisonous yellow oleander seeds into the Panchayat well and accused us of doing it. We protested saying that if anybody would do it, it would only be the Company people. Eventually they ended up cleaning the well for us. What then? The water which seeped into the newly cleaned well had the same old bitter taste.

The *Madhyamam* newspaper supported our protest right from the beginning. It was after one year that *Mathrubhumi*'s

Veerendra Kumar Sir visited us. He had come for a meeting organised to give compensation to the widow of a Company worker. I heard from Swaminathan that Veerendra Kumar Sir spoke against the Company in the very same meeting organised by the Company. When he came to the protest pandal after the meeting, we gave him water from the well to taste. He realised the full extent of our suffering only after tasting the water. From that day onwards, he and his *Mathrubhumi* paper have been there with us on all occasions. When I went to Dehradun at the invitation of Vandana Shiva, Sir gave me his car to go around the place. One day I went to Shoranur to give a talk in a school. That is where I met Veerendra Kumar Sir, who was at the time undergoing treatment in the Vaidyamadam. He reassured me even then that his and *Mathrubhumi*'s support would always be with us.

When the protest completed its thousandth day, a big meeting took place. A lot of people came to attend it. But I was not able to meet any of them. While returning from Mumbai, I fell seriously ill. On the way back home, it was Neelakantan Sir who took me to a hospital in Shoranur. I was bedridden for a week. It was then that the World Water Meeting was held. It was a three-day event. Vandana Shiva was also a participant. She is a woman of great character. She told us a lot of things in her language, which Ramdas translated for us.

Once I was invited to a meeting on the topic of agricultural seeds. After all, in the olden days, we used to cultivate many traditional paddy crops. I heard that the Government was trying to wipe out those traditional seed varieties. The Government wanted us to use only those seeds that it had made. I was invited to speak about this issue. When I got there, I found that many of our traditional seed varieties were still being preserved. Nowadays our agricultural practices have changed totally. Even the rainfall patterns are no longer the same. The water we get has also become polluted. Also the new seeds do not have the beneficial qualities of the old ones. On the whole, agriculture has been totally destroyed in our country. Modern chemical fertilisers are not good for the soil. In my speech I pointed out that traditional organic fertilisers like cowdung, goat droppings and decayed leaves were the best. The meeting took place in Dehradun. Shaji, Sarasal's son Murugan and Ramadas had all come with me for the meeting.

I had been to Mumbai before that. I was amazed to hear that adivasis in those places were beaten up like cattle and made to work like slaves even now. They captured all of us on 'cilima'. They had put up posters about the Plachimada protest all along the way and on the dais. Tears welled up in my eyes when I saw my fellow adivasis lift up my photograph on stage. Vandana Shiva and Medha Patkar had also come to that meeting.

I was able to go around a lot of places in Delhi and Mumbai. I saw the sea, misty mountains, India Gate, Gangotri, the resting place of Mahatma Gandhi, and the place where Indira Gandhi was shot. Veerendra Kumar Sir also arranged for a meeting with the President of India.

I was struck that such a great man was willing to speak to poor people like us. We went to the Parliament House hoping to meet Sonia Gandhi. It took two or three days to get a letter of permission to meet her. Despite that, we could not meet her. When we were sitting in a group, I saw her arrive at a distance. For some reason she got up and left immediately. They are important people, aren't they? Can we run up to them, hold their hands and speak to them? Moreover, I did not know the language.

I later heard from Veerendra Kumar Sir that she was sorry not to have met me.

I heard that Sonia Gandhi was coming to Plachimada one day. If I am able to see her and speak to her, I do not have much to ask her for. Just this one thing: "There is a small well in front of my house. All these days, we were drinking water from that well. Now the water is not good. We are not against you giving any company a permit or an award. But can you bring the good water back to our well?"

FIFTEEN

The Protest: Mixed Reactions

Pappamma, who sat in the protest pandal all twenty-four hours of the day, died last year. Poor thing! She would walk unsteadily as if she would fall down any moment.

Although her body was not strong, she was always in high spirits. One night when she got up to urinate, she tripped over a stone and fell. She was bedridden for two months with pain in her legs. She died in her sickbed.

Pappamma and I got ourselves photographed standing near the lake where the Company factory stood. I still have the photograph at home.

Since Pappamma's husband had died long back, we did an ordinary puja with bananas and coconuts, sprinkled turmeric water on her corpse and buried it.

Whether the wife died while the husband was alive, or the husband passed away while the wife was still living, we had special rituals for every occasion in our clan. If someone died, the womenfolk would lament and sing the *oppari* with their hair all spread out, like the Tamil people did:

The oleander bush
outside the house
planted by
the lady with abundant hair
has flowers
as bright as gold coins.
Had our lady with abundant hair
been here today
there would be abundant shade

and thronging crowds
outside.
Alas! Our lady with abundant hair
has closed her eyes.
We will lose the abundant shade
and thronging crowds
outside!

If the daughter would sing this oppari for the mother, the daughter-in-law would sing a different lament altogether:

Where did my aunt go?
The multicoloured parrot
who bought me
giving away her money?
We have lost
our multicoloured mother-parrot,
the minister of our house,
our mother!

Similarly there was also the ritual of cutting a woman's thali when her husband died. The dead man and his wife would be bathed in seven pots of water each. They would then be made to sit down clothed in their wedding finery and given betel leaves and areca nuts. Relatives like the elder brother or the younger one would cut the thali thread from the woman's neck and tie it around the dead man's neck. The female relatives would pound raw paddy grains and stuff it into the dead man's mouth. They would remove the woman's *pottu* and flowers and dress her in a white saree. If the woman died while her husband was still alive, the husband would merely cut a thread in the thali.

This is how all men and women die. In this brief interval on earth, how many fights are fought about money, the superior and the inferior, the Tamilian and the Malayali?

One day Panchami came running to me, quivering with anger. A pamphlet about a meeting to be held in Thrissur, where Prasad Sir was going to speak, was to be given to Ward Member Varadettan. Apparently, it was given to Varadettan's neighbour who was asked to pass it on to Varadettan. The

IMAGE 6: Mayilamma's arrest during the Plachimada protest.

Source: Courtesy, *Mathrubhumi* archives.

man could have simply said no; instead he picked a fight with Panchami. We heard that the Company people were again going to bring water in tankers to the Colony as per the court order. We wondered if we should accept that water considering what we had so far gone through. We announced that we would block the water tankers if the Company tried sending water to the Colony again. Varadettan's neighbour was angry about this decision. His question was: what was it that we were really fighting for? He also said that he was willing to launch a counter-protest because he believed that we would learn a lesson only if the Company was opened. According to him, refusing the Company's water amounted to an act of arrogance. Panchami gave him a piece of her mind before leaving. We were asked to sign a declaration stating that we would not oppose the Company sending water to the Colony. But what if we turned sympathetic and signed the notice after drinking the Company's water for four days?

Sarasal's story was similar. Some worker in the Company who passed by the protest pandal every day—Thaiyal's daughter would jokingly refer to him as "CID Annan"—said that if he got a respectable job in the Company, the first thing he would do is break the legs of the protesters!

Some people are like this. There are also other kinds of people. When I went to a meeting in Palakkad, a man said, "Who is this Mayilamma? In the days to come it will not be easy to meet her. She is going to become a big person!" When I heard that, I felt really embarrassed. I felt like saying to him, "No, please don't taunt me like this!" To tell you the truth, one has to be equally wary of those who praise you to the skies and those who try to trample you to dust. God! Why does it not occur to them that I am also a human being just like them?

SIXTEEN

'The Struggle for Freedom'

Quite a few court cases were filed against the protesters. One case was filed because we had dumped the fertiliser in front of the Company's gates. Two or three more were filed because we had stopped the Company's water tanker. There were two cases registered for raising slogans against the Company from a jeep. Venuettan was the first accused in two or three cases.

MLA Krishnan Kuttyettan was the first to arrange for water supply to the Company at a time when he was not aware of its double-dealings. But he stopped afterwards. Then they brought water from places like Elapully, Kozhinjampara, Outtara and Para. We blocked that too. Two cases were filed for that. In one of those cases thirty-one people were named as offenders. The other one was filed against Murugaraj, Shaktivel and Sundaran. One hundred and fourteen people had a case registered in their names for dumping fertiliser in front of the Company's gate. Eleven people were charged in the sloganeering case. Somehow no case has been filed against me till now. They must have considered me an ordinary housewife who was capable of only making gruel in the kitchen. But I do not fear a bad name like other women and speak my mind without any hesitation. This is the only reason why everyone invites Mayilamma to speak.

Papers relating to court cases would be sent to us every now and then. We could not go to work that day. One also needed money to attend to legal matters. People who came to the protest pandal would donate some money. We were able to erect cement pillars for the protest pandal with the three thousand rupees donated by a couple from Kashmir. We were also able to thatch the pandal roof with that money. People who went to work would leave two rupees as a kind of offering in the pandal. If we were really short of money, only a few of us would stay back in the pandal whereas the majority would go out to work. It has been nearly three years since we bought new clothes. In the early days of the protest, the Ayyankali Pada would collect rice and pulses for us. Later when they indulged in violence, we got scared. Poor people! They too have been charged with cases.

It has been three and a half years since we began the protest. Everyone assured us that they would be with us. We are quite happy about that. However, we still feel bad about one thing. If whatever we did and are doing is just, why is it that no one has taken any effort to stop the Company's functioning or close it down? We live in fear even now. Whenever we see a lorry enter the Company's premises, we get suspicious that the work is going to begin again.

The fourth Independence Day since the beginning of the protest has also arrived. As usual, we hoisted the national flag in the Anganwadi. *Payasam* was prepared and distributed to the children. Policemen roamed around in all places that day. We heard that the Yuvajana Vedi people had planned a demonstration to besiege the Company. Suspecting that the children would get scared, I asked the teacher to lock the Anganwadi. There were policemen inside the Anganwadi also.

Everything happened as I had feared. When the protesters went up to the gates of the Company and raised slogans, they were ruthlessly lathi-charged. The crowd dispersed and ran helter-skelter. All this was filmed by the TV people.

I feel both happy and pained when I think of the number of people who are willing to suffer for our sake. Although the story of our fight has reached far and wide and has become a burning topic, the Government still keeps mum. Apparently, the adivasis are a headache to them! If we are a headache to them, who then is not a headache? What is the reason for this headache in the first place? If only they had taken the right decision, there would not have been any reason for a headache, I think.

What is the point in saying that we are free if the land, water and air over which we have the right are not freely available to us? We are all slaves even now. Will eating sweets, planting the flag and shouting 'Jai! Jai!'[4] mean freedom?

Is not ours the land of distinguished politicians? We feel that they can easily resolve this issue if they want to. Then why is it that no conclusion is ever reached? Besides, unlike others, we are ruled by people belonging to three different parties—that of Krishnettan, Krishnadasettan and Achuvettan. If these three get together and take a unanimous decision, will it take long for the Company to close down?

I am not blaming anyone. Please do not get us wrong. We have a doubt in our minds, and our lives are without any certainties. That is why I talk about all this. We believe that you who have the brains, education and awareness that we tribal people lack would take care of our matters. We feel despair when we look back at our long journey. When we look ahead, we feel the same distress. Sometimes I wonder who is there for us now. From which part of the land will a strong, helping hand emerge?

People come to invite me from different places. I went to Thrissur to talk about the hassles of pig rearing. I went to inaugurate the mosquito eradication drive organised by a group which calls itself *Munnottu*. I also went to places like Nainamkonam, Thiruvananthapuram and Kozhikode.

Whatever it is, I know only one thing. This tiny piece of earth where I stay, Plachimada, is my home. Unbearable problems have made the place unliveable for my people. What can we do now? Where can we go running away from here? I had gone to meet Medha Patkar when she came down to Thiruvananthapuram. When I went on a hunger strike for nine days, many people came to see me. But I felt that there was no point in so many visiting me and projecting me as an

[4] Victory! Used as an expression of praise or support, especially in slogans.

important person. I was not the problem! Everyone needed to know about the condition of my place. All they needed to understand was how the well water in my house and in the houses of my people had gone bad. They needed to see for themselves how parched the farmers' lands had become in our place. For all this to happen it is better that I stay back in Plachimada. I need to bring my people together for this cause. We should not resort to blows, kicks and violence. This struggle may succeed or not. Be it life or death, we are all in it together. Till either of these happens, we will have to stand together. This is not the first time that earth and water are being destroyed, but people tell us that this is the first protest of its kind. If that is the case, we must seek an end to the problem here itself. We will be happy if it ends well. We will take it as a deserving reward for our fight. On the other hand, if we lose the struggle, the story of Plachimada will remain a lesson to all. This is not just my hope but also the desire of my people and all our well-wishers.

A DARK NIGHT'S POEM

By Jothibai Pariyadath

Saturday, 5 January 2007. It was the day nearly fifty families had chosen for a get-together to celebrate New Year. Although it was a small function, I had a million insignificant things to do as the convenor of the cultural programme and so was really tired by the end of the day. By the time the programme ended at night, the deafening blast of sound from the loudspeakers and the flashes of the ever-changing lights on the stage had triggered my migraine. When I reached home at ten in the night, the migraine had started throbbing and dancing inside my head like a snake with a raised hood. I popped a pill in an effort to subdue the headache and was trying to get some sleep in a dark room. It was then that my friend Beena from *Mathrubhumi* called to tell me that Mayilamma was no more.

What would be the first emotion when news of death forcefully raps on a closed door and opens the floodgates of memory with a start?

From the day I was introduced to Mayilamma to the last time that I saw her, these memories flashed like scenes on the screen of my mind: the day I decided to listen to her life's story and record it in words, the day I first met her, the indifferent tenor of that first meeting, memories of sitting together and sharing food in the Plachimada pandal, our trip together to Muthalamada in Attayampathy which was Mayilamma's birthplace, and the warmth with which she introduced me to her childhood friends. The image of a woman who welcomed me to sit on the mat in the verandah of her house when I went to invite her for the book release, swallowing her pain with a smile despite ill health, loneliness and the ache of neglect and the typical adivasi gumption and determination with which she spoke during the book release function—my mind was saturated with all these memories.

In the middle of this, there was yet another call from *Mathrubhumi*. As the transcriber of Mayilamma's life narrative, I was asked to come up with an impromptu obituary note.

The news of her death had begun appearing as flash news on all television channels. Her face bearing the marks of psoriasis was shown on the screen. I wished I had not seen that. The last time that I spoke to her was on 13 October 2006, the day we recorded an interview for All India Radio, Thrissur. She called me again when the interview was broadcast. She said that she was not keeping well. Her voice sounded very tired. I thought even then that the exhaustion of her mind might have affected her body as well. When I heard that she was afflicted with psoriasis and had begun treatment, I never imagined for a moment that it would be serious enough to be the cause of her death.

The night was coming to a close. It was the time when a poem sprang from within, drenching my inner being. A poem emerged after many years. No, a life! The life-story of many Mayilammas. It felt as though I was writing it, listening to her. Was I writing this, too, after listening to her? I am not sure. Words and lines arranged themselves effortlessly. I finished the poem except the last few lines before sunrise. The poem was completed in the evening when I got home after the burial rites. When I saw her face for the last time, I noticed that there was a bright glance hiding behind those closed eyelids. It was the unblinking stare of the 'eye' of the peacock feather that had always been a cause of fear for me. This also happens to be the title of my poem.

Translated by
Swarnalatha Rangarajan and **Sreejith Varma**

THE UNBLINKING EYE OF THE PEACOCK FEATHER

By Jothibai Pariyadath

Lake-side,
The indigo thicket,
The unblinking eye of the leopard,
The gleaming bronze pot
scoured by red bricks,
The noisy chatter
of bangles on the hand,
The glittering, rolled gold nosepin,
The dark-coloured, dotted saree,
Ringing anklets around the ankle,
Mayilalu, Pappalu, Valli, Muniyamma...

Around the Colony well
The women's Panchayat.[5]
The story of Kannayan's daughter
coming of age.
The swagger of Nakelan's wife
who has studied up to class four.
Chinnathayi
going to work in the Company.
In the coconut grove
The flashing eye of the leopard.
Mayilalu, Muniyamma, Valli.

Noon.
The long road,

[5] Here, gossip.

The glimmer of sweat
on the tiny nosepin,
The noisy chatter
of the bronze pots,
Beyond the palm forests,
The flicking tail of the leopard.
Mayilalu, Muniyamma ...

Along the long road,
The serpentine line
of bronze pots.
Saree-cradles and lullabies.
Outside the pandal,
The crouching feet of the leopard.
Mayilalu ...

At the foot of the big tree,
The wide eye of the leopard,
The wide, unblinking eye of the feather,
The wide, unblinking eye of the peacock feather,
Pappalu, Valli, Muniyamma ...

Translated by
Swarnalatha Rangarajan and **Sreejith Varma**

NOTES FROM PLACHIMADA

Mayilamma's life narrative springs from a blood-and-bones knowledge of place. Therefore, I felt that it was important to engage with the soil of Plachimada and its people while undertaking this translation. I wanted to 'see' things as they existed in their reality and perhaps also wanted to partake of Mayilamma's way of knowing the place, although nine years had passed since her death.

My visit to Plachimada coincided with an important ritual for Mayilamma's family—the commemorative rites of her death anniversary which falls on 6 January.

I had for company Jothibai Pariyadath, the collaborative transcriber-author of *Mayilamma*, who was familiar with Plachimada and Mayilamma's family. A chat with Jothibai on our way to Vijayanagar Colony in Plachimada prepared me for the reality of the modernising tribals who can no longer be romanticised as primitive people living in the lap of nature. Jothibai warned me, "The adivasi Colony looks like any regular working class family neighbourhood in Palakkad! So, don't expect anything exotic!"

Our first stop was in front of the Coca-Cola Bottling Plant in Plachimada that had shut down. A carpet of paddy and areca nuts was spread in front of the gates. The main signboard at the closed entrance wore a faded look. The protest pandal which had been the epicentre of all action was deserted. I was struck by the sense of desolation all around and looked around for someone to speak to. There was a small thatched haircutting saloon made from plaited coconut leaves next to the protest pandal. I noticed that a couple of men from the saloon were watching us. One of them seemed willing to talk to us. Jothibai and I asked him about the protest. He told us that he had been born and brought up in Plachimada. He was in complete denial, saying that the whole Plachimada issue was just a culmination of labourers' disagreement with the Company, and that there was never any problem with water. He seemed suspicious of us and kept on enquiring if we were from the media. I encountered the same mistrust when I went to the shop adjacent to the protest pandal to buy a few sheets of white paper. The woman who was taking care of the store was reluctant to part with the paper sheets. I had to convince her that I was just a visitor to Plachimada and not a media person. Finally, a man who appeared to be her husband had to intervene and get her to agree to give me the paper sheets.

At this juncture, I pondered at length about the way to 'know' Plachimada, about how to activate and reactivate the complex articulations and relations to things. I was frankly puzzled by the ambiguities that greeted me in almost every corner. Was this the place of hope that had set the limits to corporate greed, a site which demonstrated 'globalisation from below' by linking the local, national and the global? Or was I walking in the midst of the ghosts of Plachimada – a place that had slipped into oblivion and cynicism after the passing away of its charismatic leader, Mayilamma? The landscape also seemed to be resolute in hiding its secrets. The swaying palm trees and the pockets of dense thickets which dotted the place did not give me the sense of a wounded landscape.

The next stop was Mayilamma's home. It was a humble Colony house with a tiled roof. Although I did not go inside, I could see that the house was in bad shape. The wooden doors were chipped and termite-eaten in places; the lime-washed walls bore cracks and crevices where the bricks had crumbled.

We met Thangavelu, Mayilamma's second son, in the front yard which was bare except for a few flowering plants. He and his wife Mini pointed to the well on the left side of the house – the iconic well which had presaged the environmental troubles of Plachimada. The well had water, but Mini said that it remained unusable. Thangavelu sounded more optimistic and said that the water quality seemed to be improving. Soon

Mayilamma's daughter Deivana and her younger brother Supramani also joined us, although they did not participate much in the conversation. It was a happy gathering of Mayilamma's children and grandchildren who answered my questions with great courtesy and willingly posed for photographs. I also got to visit the neighbour's house where mineral water cans were being unloaded from a truck. They said that they used mineral water to drink. They also told me that they had sealed the well in their backyard because they did not believe that the water would ever get better. As I was leaving, Mayilamma's family asked me to accompany them for the ritual near Mayilamma's grave the next day.

The next morning, I reached the Colony rather early in the day. I was curious to see the Anganwadi and the adivasi children studying there who were central to Mayilamma's concerns in the opening chapter of her life narrative. There was still some time left for the Anganwadi to open. The Anganwadi Centre No. 82 was a small building with a low tiled roof, bare but for a swing outside that was missing a seat. I wondered if it was symbolic of the reality of the lives of the children who studied there. A woman from the neighbouring house came out on seeing me. She chit-chatted for a while and I thought I would ask her about Chella, the helper who comes under fire in the first chapter of the narrative for preparing undercooked gruel for the children. "Oh, Chella! She is gone! Died of AIDS," she said matter-of-factly. Plachimada appeared to have many layers of dis-ease! By that time, the teacher of the Anganwadi had also come. I chatted with her as we stepped into the Anganwadi. When I asked her if the school was exclusively for adivasi children, she said that children from adivasi as well as other communities came to the Centre. When I enquired about the daily food provided to the children, she rattled off the menu for the entire week which sounded wholesome. The classroom was gaily festooned with charts and pictures. The children appeared happy. As I left the place I thought to myself that Mayilamma's battle was perhaps about the importance of keeping basic things going well.

Mayilamma's family was waiting for me. I met Murugaraj, the eldest son of Mayilamma, who was not present the day before. We were also joined by Mariyappan, the President of the Adivasi Samrakshana Sangham. After travelling for a while over a tarred road, our car entered a mud path that ensured a bumpy ride from there onwards. The road was flanked by wild thickets and we stopped on the bridge under which the waters of the Kamabalathara lake gushed forth. The lake looked clear since it was fed by the water coming from dams in the vicinity. Vilayodi Venugopal, along with a few other local people, was already waiting for us at the cemetery. The graveyard was a small space cleared out in the thicket. The grave was a small mound of earth; a frail *tulasi* plant growing on top of the mound was the only memorial marker.

Mildly put, I was taken aback to see the state of Mayilamma's grave. I was told that there were plans to construct a proper memorial on the spot. The graves of Mayilamma and Velur Swaminathan, another important face of the Plachimada struggle, were adjacent to each other. The ritual resonated with the stark simplicity of the place. A lamp, joss sticks and camphor were lit in front of the grave. There was no ritual chanting of any kind. A coconut was broken and offered to the departed. Garlands were also placed on the graves of both Mayilamma and Velur Swaminathan. We, along with the members of the family, circumambulated the grave with joined palms. We then took a pinch of the sacred ash which was heaped on the grave—a symbol of benediction from the dead.

On my way back to the protest pandal to begin the interview with Vilayodi Venugopal, I knew that I had experienced something bare and sacred—the lives of the poor. The silence enveloping Mayilamma's grave seemed to chant the powerful lines from her narrative: "*What is the point in saying that we are free if the land, water and air over which we have the right are not freely available to us*?" Did Mayilamma win her battle? The answer, perhaps, is not a resounding yes. As I was going home after the interview, I noticed the lone banana plant with its cluster of fruit standing in sentinel-like fashion outside the protest pandal. It reminded me of Mayilamma and the great power of lone eco-warriors.

'I NEVER DREAMT I WOULD WRITE AN IMPORTANT BOOK LIKE THIS!'

An Interview with Jothibai Pariyadath

Jothibai Pariyadath, the transcriber of Mayilamma's life narrative, is an acclaimed poet in Malayalam. Her first poetry collection titled, *Pesamadantha*, was published in 2009. She has also brought out the Malayalam translation of the poems of the Russian poet, Vladimir Mayakovsky, as *Mayakovskyude Kavithakal* (2012) as well as the Malayalam translation, along with P. S. Manoj Kumar, of the script (2008) of the Italian film, *La Notte* (1961) directed by Michelangelo Antonioni. She became the first female editor of a Malayalam online literary magazine when she launched *Jyothis* in 2005. Pariyadath's blog, *Kavyam Sugeyam*, which was started in 2005 featuring the recitations, in her mellifluous voice, of more than five hundred Malayalam poems by poets spanning multiple generations, is hugely popular among Malayalam poetry lovers and has more than seven hundred followers. She is the recipient of 'Bhasha Sevana Puraskaram' by the Palakkad District Panchayat and the Coimbatore Kerala Cultural Centre's literary prize in 2012.

Mayilamma's life narrative is also a testimony. It has the significance of chronicling the life of a woman belonging to the voice-less, subaltern community. Equally important, I feel, are the many environmental concerns raised by the text. Mayilamma: Oru Jeevitham *easily belongs to the genre of environmental justice non-fiction that foregrounds the dangers of myopic, greed-driven and ecologically destructive industrial ventures. In fact, there is a surge in the publication of such ecojustice narratives in various world languages. How do you personally think Mayilamma's life story would contribute to the body of such ecojustice narratives?*

I think *Mayilamma: Oru Jeevitham* captures the essence of environmental justice literature in every sense of that term. I would also say that Mayilamma's story deserves to be included in that category, because it is not just the story of an exceptional individual called Mayilamma; on the contrary, it is the story of many unsung Mayilammas. I have pointed this out in my poem on Mayilamma titled, 'Mayilppeeli Thurukannu' [The Unblinking Eye of the Peacock Feather]. When one Mayilamma passes away, many more Mayilammas are born. Those who become Mayilammas by dint of their efforts and passion, and those who are forced to become Mayilammas! I am of the opinion that the injustice borne by Mayilamma and her people is on par with the injustice done to the land and natural resources of Plachimada. Mayilamma didn't get justice. In my poem, I have offered my subjective take on Mayilamma.

'Mayilppeeli Thurukannu' is truly a remarkable poem. Could you tell me a little more about it?

Thank you! The poem was written in the night, when I returned home after attending Mayilamma's last rites. You could see a pattern in the way every stanza ends. The last line of every stanza comprises just the names of the adivasi women, but the number of people mentioned changes every time. The name, 'Mayilalu' [Mayilamma], however, is present till the third stanza before disappearing in the last one. This signifies the passing away of Mayilamma. After death, her body was placed at the foot of a tree outside the Company gate, which too is indicated in the last stanza of the poem. The poem also employs animal imagery—that of a prowling leopard, which takes on the added connotation of the Coca-Cola Company as the poem develops, while the peacock's feather obviously refers to Mayilamma ['Mayil' is the Malayalam word for peacock]. The stare of a stalking leopard, of course, is frightening. The image of a peacock's feather, or a peacock for that matter, may look rather feeble when compared to the leopard's. But there is this remarkable quality to a peacock's feather that if you look at its 'eye' for a while, you will get transfixed and perhaps a little frightened as well! The poem also describes the transition in the lives of the women of Plachimada from fetching water from the well to waiting with pots in long queues under the hot noon sun for water distributed from the tankers. I have received a lot of appreciation for that poem. I especially prize the writer Methil Radhakrishnan's praise for that poem.

A host of adivasi and Dalit movements are taking place in Kerala with the objective of forcefully asserting the indigenous communities' rights to the land and water commons. How would you situate the predominantly adivasi-led struggle in Plachimada within this larger picture of indigenous struggles in Kerala?

What is *prakriti*? The land, air and water. Any activity that pollutes these should be understood within the context of the exploitation of nature. Moreover, it was when the globalising forces were facing extreme forms of opposition that the campaign against a corporate giant like Coca-Cola was kick-started in Plachimada. Though the struggle was begun mostly by the adivasis, later on the whole local population of Plachimada rallied around them. It shaped up as a local people's movement against a global corporate. To a large extent, politics and politicians were not involved in the movement then. Politicians began to intervene in the affairs only later. It was, as Mayilamma herself highlights in the book, truly a David-Goliath kind of struggle in Plachimada against the phenomena of globalisation and imprudent privatisation.

How would you describe Mayilamma as a person and as a leader?

I didn't have an opportunity to see her as a leader in action. I first met her after the Coca-Cola Company was shut down. The Mayilamma I met was a remarkable person. Innocent and rustic. If you visit the border rural areas of Palakkad district, you would come across such women irrespective of their caste or religion. Those simple women would talk and behave exactly like her. The Malayalam they speak has a strong Tamil flavour. I am convinced that Mayilamma had good leadership qualities. I got a whiff of it during my conversations with her. I saw her on the dais only twice. The first time was during the release of this book and the second, when she came to inaugurate a function in Palakkad conducted by an organisation called Munnottu. She didn't speak much on the latter occasion. But when she spoke, her voice always pulsated with anger against the exploitation of nature and the pollution of water in our courtyard-wells.

Do you feel that Mayilamma was aware that she was becoming a symbol of the grassroots anti-globalisation movements that are happening across the world?

I am not sure she understood that in the early days of her campaign. But later, I am sure that Mayilamma did understand what she was standing for when she was invited to different places and shared some important platforms like the World Water Conference with activists like Vandana Shiva, and also, when others began to give her respect and consideration as a movement leader. One could notice that in her demeanour and approach. Even during our discussions for the writing of the book, she explained things with the same passion.

Is there a memorable incident or a scenario where you witnessed extraordinary suffering during your visits to Plachimada that you may want to share with us – something that is not included in the book?

I used to catch a bus to Plachimada and go straight to the protest pandal. As for the problems like poverty or the lack of clothing, one could only imagine what they were going through. When you saw her tired face, you could tell that she must have skipped her previous meal that day. The one specific affliction that I witnessed was disease. When we were sitting in the pandal, I had seen mothers bringing in their sick children to see Mayilamma. She would enquire about their health and refer them to hospitals and doctors to be consulted. As I mentioned before, I first visited Plachimada in June 2005. The Company officially closed down in 2004. But I knew that there were still people inside the plant. I don't know what was going on inside the Company gates, but the villagers told me that it was still running. Perhaps it was only an expression of the local people's deep-seated suspicion about the Company. Another routine sight was the long queue of people carrying their pots to fetch drinking water that was distributed in tankers. What struck me the most, however, was the neatness of their *ooru*.[6] I am not sure how many of us 'outsiders' would imagine or expect adivasi streets to be so clean. The streets of Vijaynagar Colony, the Anganwadi, all were very well maintained. The parapets of the Panchayat well were neatly whitewashed. Only the water inside the well was dirty. People couldn't stop talking about the contaminated water in the wells. When I visited the children in the Anganwadi, I realised that even the songs that they were taught described the village's colossal environmental tragedy. Thus, even though I wasn't a part of the campaign from its beginning, I understood their sufferings through my interactions with them.

By then, the adivasi land rights activist C. K. Janu's life narrative, Janu: C. K. Januvinte Jeevitha Katha *[Janu: C. K. Janu's Life-story] (2002) had been published. So were the Dalit ecoactivist Kallen Pokkudan's first autobiography,* Kandalkkadukalkkidayil Ente Jeevitham *[My Life Amidst the Mangrove Forests] (2002) and Nalini Jameela's best-selling,* Oru Lyngiga Thozhilaliyude Athmakatha *[The Autobiography of a Sex Worker] (2005), to name a few. The life narratives of people from the subaltern/marginalised groups were becoming a sort of a new literary fad in Malayalam then. The publication of Mayilamma's life narrative came close on their heels, didn't it?*

That is right. But, you see, I wasn't planning to come up with a life narrative. Besides, I wasn't that popular as a writer back then. I used to write poems. Some of them had got published. I hadn't stepped outside that small circle.

How do you think the readers responded to Mayilamma: Oru Jeevitham*? You might have had certain objectives in your mind while writing a book like this. Do you think they have been met?*

To be frank, I hadn't set any specific aim or objective while writing this book. I got an invitation from *Mathrubhumi* to prepare the life narrative of Mayilamma. At thirty-nine years of

---

[6] A tribal settlement.

age, I never dreamt I would write an important book like this! When I was done, I read out the entire draft to Mayilamma and gave it for publication only after getting her approval.

But in hindsight, do you feel that Mayilamma: Oru Jeevitham, *which was published at a time when life-writings were rather in vogue in Malayalam, didn't get its due attention, both popular and critical?*

I don't even know if I could really call this book 'mine,' for the book's first edition was presented as though it was *written* by Mayilamma herself! Perhaps, going by today's literary conventions, a 'transcriber' should expect only that much, no matter how much diligence, dedication and imagination you might display in your work! Yes, there are certain restraints to be exercised while putting to use one's imagination in writing someone else's real life story. But, from my writing experience, I have learned that wise use of one's imagination is also required in the process. Unfortunately, in spite of all your toil, the translators and transcribers are always accorded a second-class status.

Coming back to your question about the readers' response to the book, the book went into two editions. A thousand copies were printed for the first edition and I heard that they were sold out quickly. One day, I received a phone call from a college professor who informed me that the book was included in the cultural studies course syllabus of MA in Malayalam at Kannur University. But no copies of the book were available in the market and he called me to enquire if I could give him at least one copy! I was thrilled to know that the book was included by Kannur University in its syllabus. I thought it was an honour to be recognised by the university like that. Later, I learned that the book was also included in an undergraduate course offered by the University of Calicut. I don't know if it's still used as a textbook there. When I realised the state of affairs, I called up *Mathrubhumi* and requested them to bring out a second edition. At the same time, I felt that the second edition wouldn't be interesting if it didn't carry any updates on the life-story of Mayilamma. So, I decided to append to the book a brief note of my experiences on the day of Mayilamma's death along with my poem.

The Coca-Cola Company in Plachimada was shut down in March 2004. The first edition of Mayilamma: Oru Jeevitham *was published in 2006. But the details of the post-shutdown phase of the Plachimada movement that one might expect to find in the book were not included in it. Do you think including those details could have made the book more comprehensive?*

As I mentioned earlier, I was only a poet then. It goes without saying that there is a world of difference between writing a prose work and a poem. I didn't have any experience or practice of writing elaborate and detailed prose pieces. So, *Mayilamma: Oru Jeevitham*, admittedly, has all such little—and perhaps big—lapses that one might find in anybody's first book.

But you could have included those details in the book's second edition?

I did want to do that for the second edition. But my writing got delayed. And one day, totally out of the blue, I heard this news that the book was used as a textbook by the Kannur University. When I was informed about it, I was at a physiotherapy centre, undergoing treatment since I wasn't keeping well. So, I couldn't go to Plachimada and do the required study to prepare the updates for the second edition. I really wanted to do that. I will certainly make those additions in the book's next edition.

How did the book's Tamil translation happen? How did they find this book and how did they get interested in the translation project?

The Tamil translators told me that somebody had suggested the book to them. I can't read Tamil, but I follow spoken Tamil. They came to see me saying that they had already done the translation! They read out the first two pages of their translation. Later I heard that the book's Tamil translation featured in the list of the ten best Tamil books published that year. So I guess it must be a good translation.

You are a translator yourself. You have translated Vladimir Mayakovsky's poems into Malayalam. How do you go about the translation process?

I read and re-read the text and meditate on words to find the most appropriate ones. When I translated Mayakovsky's poems into Malayalam, I had gone into a frenzy in mentally hunting for the right words. I have also translated a script into Malayalam. Translating a script is less taxing in comparison with the task of translating poetry. I think translating a book like *Mayilamma: Oru Jeevitham,* that employs an oral style of narration, calls for an extended meditation on words to choose the most appropriate ones.

As you have rightly pointed out, one of the striking features of this book is its oral narrative style, appropriately marked by the earthiness of the adivasi tongue. I feel that it helps the book to establish a more intimate relationship with its readers.

That is right!

You visited Plachimada at the height of the agitation. Many years later, you have again visited the place today. Did you notice any notable changes in the adivasis' environmental outlook or, in general, their way of life?

A major change that struck me on my visit today was that the womenfolk have also started going to work. Previously, the women used to sit in the pandal and only the men would go to work. So the pandal was mostly populated by women. But today I found that the pandal was deserted.

The cause of Mayilamma's death was the disease psoriasis. But S. Faisy, in her preface to the second edition of Mayilamma: Oru Jeevitham, *had noted that Mayilamma's death was due to "her disease exacerbated by the environmental problems [in Plachimada]." Today, when we spoke to Mayilamma's children, they said that she caught the disease from a wound that developed after she hit her head on the palm-leaf roof of a cattle barn.*

Yes, Mayilamma's children seem to believe so. People would come up with different reasons like this. But in my opinion, mental turmoil always worsens psoriasis, or any disease for that matter. Mayilamma was going through a lot of stress and anguish during that time.

Once, during one of our conversations, you hinted that Mayilamma had faced a few instances of moral policing. What were they?

Those were mentioned to me by Mayilamma herself. As stated in the book, she was widowed at a young age. The morality-related questions faced by young widows in our society are quite predictable. Mayilamma spoke about it only in that way. But she was pretty upset when she told me that despite being the old woman that she was then, there were still people who raised questions about her morality. However, I didn't want to delve deep into it. As a woman myself, I felt it would be a little insensitive if I asked her more about it. I just couldn't do it.

'AFTER A BATH, ONE WOULD FEEL GIDDY—AS IF THERE WAS A HEAVY LOAD ON THE HEAD!'

An Interview with Mayilamma's son, Thangavelu, and his wife, Mini

Do you hope that the quality of the well water will improve?

Thangavelu: No, not in the near future. I do not know how many generations would have to wait for that to happen.

Is it really because of the Company's activities that the water got polluted?

Mini: When I came here after my marriage, there was no problem about water. When I went back home for my delivery, the water was still good here. Everyone from the Plachimada Colony used to come here to draw water for bathing and washing clothes. The Company was not established at that time.

So, when did you realise that the water was being contaminated?

Thangavelu: We found out that the quality of water was worsening within six months of the Company's functioning.

From where did you fetch water when the well water became polluted?

Thangavelu: From Kochikkad.

How far is Kochikkad from here?

Thangavelu: It is quite far. On the other side of this road is Thottichippathy. Beyond that is Kochikkad. We used to bring water on bicycles. We suffered a lot then.

It is described in Mayilamma's life narrative that people caught many diseases after they came in contact with the polluted water. How do you recall those days?

Thangavelu: That is correct. Our skin would itch. After taking a bath one would feel giddy—as if there was a heavy load on the head!

You belong to the Eravallar tribe, don't you?

Thangavelu: Yes.

Are all the people in your neighbourhood Eravallar tribals?

Thangavelu: Not all of them. The Eravallars occupy houses in this street of the Colony from the third house onwards.

I saw bottles of mineral water being unloaded from a truck in the house opposite. So, the people who have the money buy those bottles to ensure they have clean water to drink?

Thangavelu: Yes. Those who can afford it buy mineral water. Others have to be content with the pipe water.

The adivasi culture is known for its close ties with nature. Would you like to comment about that?

Thangavelu: I have heard that my grandmother's generation used to lead such a way of life. As children, we still had access to the remnants of this lifestyle—mainly through our games. We did live like that once upon a time. But because of the so-called 'progress' and 'development,' our lifestyles have undergone changes.

Do you visit Muthalamada nowadays?

Thangavelu: It has been quite a while since I visited Muthalamada. But my elder brothers pay a visit there every now and then.

When I went to the house across the street, I learned that the women in your neighbouring house go to work in agricultural fields.

Mini: We also go to work in paddy and coconut fields. We do jobs ranging from planting rice seedlings to harvesting.

But how do you meet the water requirements for all these activities?

Mini: We do not go to work only in this village. In fact, we go to work in places very far from here—like Kozhinjampara, Chittur and Nenmara. We work on a contract basis.

Is any farming happening at all in Plachimada at present?

Mini: We are going to other places to work because it is hard to find work here. Besides, labourers are heavily in demand in other places. Whenever our contractor phones us to inform us about available work, we get going.

You must have suffered many hardships during the time of the protest. You must have not been able to go to work as usual?

Thangavelu: Yes! During the time of the protest, I went to Thrissur and worked as a construction labourer there due to our financial problems. I used to visit home every now and then. But when my mother was diagnosed with psoriasis, it was I who stayed with her in the hospital and took care of her. She had come home for just one day to attend my elder brother's *kettu nira*[7] ceremony. But she could not watch the ceremony. That was how she died.

Did she catch psoriasis because of her exposure to the contaminated water? Did her doctor mention anything like that?

Thangavelu: We had a cattle barn here that was thatched with palm leaves. Apparently, she was wounded by the sharp tips of the palm fronds. That wound left a black discolouration which then spread all over her body.

We can divide the lives of the people of Plachimada into three phases: before the setting up of the Company, during its functioning and the period when the Company was shut down. How do you compare your living conditions in these three phases?

Thangavelu: Before the coming of the Company, work was abundantly available here. There were sugarcane fields in Plachimada. I was not married then. Our hardships began after the arrival of the Company. At present, our situation is comparatively better.

---

[7]'Kettu nira' is a ceremony when the devotees who are going to visit the Lord Ayyappa Temple in Sabarimala (Kerala) prepare a travel kit called 'irumudikkettu' containing both puja articles and personal belongings.

'OUR COMMUNITY SEEMS TO BE CHANGING'

An Interview with Mariyappan

Mariyappan, a native of Govindapuram in Muthalamada Panchayat in Palakkad, is the President of the Adivasi Samrakshana Sangham [The Organisation for the Protection of Adivasis]. It was under the aegis of this organisation that the tribals of Plachimada launched their satyagraha protest on Earth Day, 22 April 2002.

What are the objectives of your organisation? Does it function only in this locality?

Yes, this organisation functions in about three or four neighbouring Panchayats. It helps those who are denied the benefits of Government welfare schemes. We help them fight for and obtain these benefits from the Government which is their rightful due. Actually, the mere fact that this organisation exists is reassuring to the adivasis here. Thanks to the Sangham, violence against the adivasis has stopped. Previously, the muthalalis would cite some reason and beat up the adivasis. Such incidents do not happen any more.

Why did Eravallar adivasis migrate from Muthalamada to Plachimada?

Our people came and settled here since the generation of my parents. In those days, our people used to work in the agricultural fields of the muthalalis. Before that, we were settled in Kalathumputhoor in Tamil Nadu when we were allotted land in Muthalamada. When we got land there, we crossed the Kerala border and settled in Muthalamada. I remember those days very well. I have attended school only up to class two. I have four siblings. When my father's income was not sufficient, my elder brother and I started going with father for work. When I worked in Muthalamada, my wage was just five rupees per month.

What did you cultivate in Muthalamada? Rice?

No. Grams, corn, ragi, *chama* and so on. Muthalamada is still known for the cultivation of these crops. Mayilamma is my relative. She got married at the age of about sixteen. There was a Gounder named Kokkemayiner. At the time of Mayilamma's marriage, her family was settled in this Gounder's compound. This Gounder owned the Kalathumputhoor land. He gave away hilly high grounds to the adivasis. That was how Mayilamma's family got the land. Their house was built in that *porambokku*[8] land. That house is still intact. When she moved to Perumatty, she let her relatives stay in that house.

Mayilamma was young when her husband Marimuthu passed away. But she did not remarry though remarriage is quite common in our community. Even those who are forty or fifty years of age get married again. But Mayilamma did not. She raised her children into independent adults. In those days, Attayampathy was occupied by our people only. 'Pathy' is the name of a neighbourhood consisting of ten Eravallar houses. Similar to what we now refer to as a 'Colony'; that is the 'pathy' in 'Attayampathy'. Muthalamada has the largest number of 'pathys': Attayampathy, Shavalampathy, Mondipathy, Chukkumpathy, Periyapathykkadu, Nappanaickerpathy, Manayarpathy, Mannadayarpathy and so on. Some 'pathys' are named after the muthalalis. There was a muthalali named 'Nappa Naicker'; 'Nappanaickerpathy' got its name from him. In Perumatty, there are Mathavamootharpathy and Kunjimenonpathy.

Is not Muthalamada nearby?

Yes. It is the neighbouring Panchayat. It is about ten kilometres from here. The largest Eravallar population is in Muthalamada.

---

[8] Waste land unfit for cultivation.

You may have heard of the Venganad Kovilakam in Kollengode. Eravallars were originally the servants of the King of Venganad Kovilakam. Wherever the Kollengode King had lands, there were only Eravallars. The Eravallars were distributed lands for cultivation by the King. But later other people stole these lands from our people. Actually, Eravallars were found to occupy land up to Munnar in Idukki district in Kerala. Eravallars were then known by a different name, Vedar. That is why we place a bow and an arrow on the occasion of a marriage. We regard the arrow as our god. We tie the thali after offering puja to the arrow. Such rituals are becoming less common nowadays. Our community seems to be changing. People have adopted more of the *savarna*[9] styles.

But do your people not regard yourselves as 'savarnas'? *For instance, I have heard that the members of your community will not allow members of other communities to touch your wells.*

The restriction to people belonging to other communities was not confined to the touching of or using our wells. Any outsider who pays us a visit was not supposed to come within a hundred metres of our houses. We consider ourselves polluted even if the brahmins entered our courtyard. We do not give water to outsiders in our household vessels. We will pour it out to their cupped hands.

How long ago are we talking about here?

I am past fifty-six years of age now. Pollution rituals were observed when I was ten to fifteen years old. During menstruation, women had to stay in isolation for seven days in a hut with a thatched roof made of coconut leaves which was built near the main house. One of the family members would keep vigil over the woman by staying just outside the hut. In those days, as you know, there were no electric lights in our village. So, we would build a fire and lie down there. After the seventh day, before the woman returned to the house, she had to take a bath. The courtyard would be smeared with cow dung. Similarly, post-delivery, the woman would not be

[9] A term used to indicate the upper castes in India.

allowed entry to the house for fifteen days. We did not consult any doctor for either pregnancy or childbirth. We had our own medicines and cures. For example, the medicine for the woman for the first month after her delivery was this: palm jaggery, dried ginger and pepper were ground in a wooden mortar (*ural*) and the powder was filled in an earthen pot. The woman had to consume this mixture within that one month. Likewise, we are divided into different clans. Members of certain clans are forbidden to marry people from certain other clans. Also, men and women would dance on the occasion of marriage. But this custom too is becoming rather uncommon these days. Recently, however, this dance was performed and some people came and recorded it on a CD. We are aware of all the rituals to be practised. But nowadays people do not bother much about following them during special occasions.

What would be the approximate population of Eravallars here?

There would be about two thousand families here [in Palakkad]. They are scattered in Panchayats like Kozhinjampara, Vadakara and Erinjampathy. But the majority of the Eravallar population is in Perumatty and Muthalamada Panchayats. They are distributed from Meenakshipuram till Ellakkad.

'ARE YOU *SANYASIS* WHO HAVE WANDERED INTO THE PROTEST?'

An Interview with Vilayodi Venugopal, Chairman of the Plachimada Anti-Coca-Cola Agitation Committee, in January 2016

The name Vilayodi Venugopal will be familiar to anyone who keenly observes the different socio-environmental battles being fought in contemporary Kerala to protect the air, water and earth as well as the rights of the indigenous communities to these commons. He is the Chairman of the Anti-Coca-Cola Agitation Committee which was instrumental in bringing together the aggrieved tribals to launch the non-violent protest against Coke in Plachimada. Venugopal's concern for human and environmental rights violations has also drawn him into active participation in people's movements like the 'Nilpu Samaram' [Standing Protest] in front of the Kerala Secretariat led by the adivasis, the infamous endosulfan pesticide disaster in Kasaragod and the recent protest against the establishment of a private airport, to name just a few. We sat down inside the protest pandal for a freewheeling chat that ran up to about one and a half hours. Excerpts:

What is the current status of the Plachimada agitation?

It is now the Government's turn to take necessary action. The Central Government has returned the Plachimada Compensation Bill to the State Government. The previous UPA Government and the NDA Government before that also had done the same. It is the responsibility of the State Government to get the honourable Governor's approval after passing the

IMAGE 7: Mayilamma with Medha Patkar.

Source: Courtesy, *Mathrubhumi* archives.

bill through voting in the Kerala Legislative Assembly. It is the State Government's responsibility to seek legal advice and confer with the Central Government, if required, to overcome difficulties in case any technicalities are involved. It also has a duty to intervene in this issue in a democratic manner.

According to some news reports that were published in 2010, a High Power Committee established by the Kerala State Government had recommended to give 216 crore rupees to the Plachimada victims. But when I asked some of the villagers here, they said that they had not got any money as compensation till date. What is the progress in the matter of compensation?

This High Power Committee was set up in 2009 and they submitted the report in 2010. On 24 February 2011, it was brought as a bill in the Kerala Legislative Assembly and was unanimously passed. In March, it was sent to the Central Government with the Governor's recommendation. However, the Central Government raised some technical issues and consulted the State Government. The State Government responded to the Central Government's queries by adhering to the Plachimada Agitation Committee's stance. Thus, those technicalities were overcome and the approval of different union ministries was also obtained. The next step involved the Union Home Minister writing a note to the President of India. Nothing much has happened since. I strongly believe that development in India should not cater only to the millionaires. Mahatma Gandhi had said that development should primarily address the needs of the poor man and that his material security should be taken care of.

How do you look at Mayilamma's leadership in the Plachimada agitation?

Mayilamma was very active in the protest. Her presence was an inspiration to other women to join the protest, especially given the fact that the local population is mostly illiterate.

How did Mayilamma rise to the leadership position of the Plachimada struggle?

That was only because of her active engagement with the issue. One naturally gains the approval of others through one's interventions.

Mayilamma did become a symbol of anti-globalisation movements. However, do you think that she has been forgotten after her death? I ask this because today I noticed that her grave is in a state of neglect.

People wonder why we are continuing with the protest even after the Company was shut down. The local, illiterate population will be content as long as they get good drinking water. They don't realise that this is a form of neo-colonisation. They have understood only to a certain extent that the Company belongs to a larger picture of capitalist forces that exploit natural resources to make profit. However, the Agitation Committee has been able to continue with its protest because of the existence of this awareness among them. Earlier, many people had said that there was no need to go on with the protest after the Company was shut down in April 2004. The fact that the State Government appointed the High Power Committee is proof that it acknowledged the stance of the Plachimada Agitation Committee as did the other political parties in Kerala. The Coca-Cola Company has caused a lot of suffering to the Plachimada villagers. The High Power Committee has enlisted about eleven crimes that the Company has committed including the violation of human rights.

Are there any NGOs functioning here at present?

No. The Solidarity Group had distributed rice to the activists in the early days of the protest. They had also built houses for four or five people here. Recently, they have offered to distribute water after digging a bore well and building a tank in the Sooryappara Colony if the drinking water supply project planned for the Colony does not materialise. Actually, I wanted this to be set up in the EMS Colony. In addition to the forty tribal families, there are about a hundred non-tribals also in that Colony. A seven-hundred-feet-deep bore well was dug there, but no water could be found. So, the Scheduled Caste Department came and closed that well. The Colony is located on a lower plane. Water runs at different levels under the earth's surface like the blood that circulates through the veins in a human body. We were able to find water, a few feet away from the bore well, at the depth of one-hundred-and-fifty feet! What I mean to say is that the underground water runs along that level there. These channels of water are literally the veins and arteries of the earth. We may not find water if we drill and dig a bore well at the same level that the Coca-Cola Company had drilled.

What was your real challenge in the early days of the Plachimada protest? Was it to mobilise the uneducated tribals and spread awareness?

One of the primary needs of man is water. The tribals began to react and got themselves involved in this issue when they began to experience the drinking water problem. As you said, they are uneducated and mostly illiterate as well. They do not know what underground water exploitation means. Nor do they have any idea about the pollution laws in the country. But at the end of the day, as the saying goes, experience is the best teacher.

As described in Mayilamma's life narrative, the tribals' uprising against a corporate giant like Coca-Cola was truly a David-Goliath kind of struggle. Were they scared about the protest in the beginning?

Yes, a sense of fear was there among them in the early days of the protest. But when more and more people intervened in this issue, they naturally gained confidence. They knew that they had to survive. They realised that they were not alone in the fight, that many others were ready to extend a helping hand.

I read an interview of yours that was published in the Keraleeyam *magazine in March 2009. In that interview, you say:* "As per the court's verdict, the Company can function even now using the Panchayat's licence. But that the Company does not operate is only because of the presence, however weak it might be, of the Agitation Committee."[10]

The Coca-Cola Company can function even now because it has the 'conditional licence'. It can operate by bringing water from outside. It had set up a treatment plant and a reverse osmosis plant and so on. The conditional licence only stipulates that the Company should not use water from this locality.

Did the environmental justice activists like Vandana Shiva and Medha Patkar visit Plachimada at your invitation?

I am one of the four state-level convenors of the National Alliance of People's Movements (NAPM) whose national convenor is Medha Patkar. So we had discussed the Plachimada issue in a meeting held in Ernakulam. Later, it was taken up for discussion in the national committee of NAPM. Afterwards, NAPM's national campaign, '*Desh Banao, Desh Bachao*' [Build the Nation, Save the Nation] march was started from Plachimada on 26 January 2003. It culminated in Ayodhya. The campaign was against cultural fascism and globalisation. Plachimada was seen as a victim of globalising forces that exploit and monopolise natural resources like water.

---

[10] Vilayodi Venugopal. 'Plachimada Vote Bankalla Rashtriya Nilapadanu,' *Keraleeyam*, March, 2010: 30-31. <http://www.keraleeyammasika.com/media/2014/04/30-31-Plachimada-Vottu-Bankalla-Rashtreeya-Nilapaadanu-March-2009.pdf>

A man called Ramadas – he is no more – from Plachimada was a part of this march till its end. He used to speak about the Plachimada struggle. The march covered about twenty states of India. That was how Plachimada got national attention. It gained wider, international attention on the occasion of the World Water Conference which was held here.

What is the status of the Pepsi Company located in Puthussery?

The Pepsi Company is located in Chullimada. Protests were carried out there also. But as per an ordinance passed by the Kerala State Government, the industrial department has wrested the Panchayat's power stating that it was an industrial site. There were cases filed in court in connection with that. The court upheld the ordinance and passed its verdict in favour of the Government. But after the Legislative Assembly committee's intervention, some guidelines were issued pertaining to the drawing of water. Because of that the Pepsi Company is operating by bringing water from other places. There are not many families living in that area. Besides, the Pepsi Company rehabilitated some of the families living in K. K. Challa (*name of a place near Palakkad*).

Do you think the Plachimada tribals could be regarded as 'developmental refugees'?

They are at once the refugees *created by* the 'development' and the *victims of* the 'development!' You see, we do need development, but not development that spells destruction.

I saw a recent newspaper report that stated that Perumatty Panchayat had become 'Kerala's first agrarian Grama Panchayat' and had waved goodbye to all kinds of industrial ventures.

That is right. It has been decided that henceforth no industrial projects will be entertained in the Panchayat. If that decision is sincere, we accept it wholeheartedly.

The ecology of Plachimada was severely damaged due to the activities of the Company. Is there any hope for restoration?

The High Power Committee has recommended that the Company should find counter methods to bring back the balance of the environment. Some positive changes have been noted in the environment of Plachimada after the Company closed down.

I saw some mineral water cans being unloaded from a truck. People said those who could afford it were buying their drinking water.

A few years ago, when we heard reports that people in some foreign countries bought drinking water in bottles, we laughed at them in contempt. Now it has become common in India. It is quite sad. We hear there are oxygen parlours in China because of pollution. We may see them in India too in the future.

Tribals of Kerala have been engaged in various struggles for their basic rights since Indian independence – like the long-drawn tribal struggle for land led by C. K. Janu. Do you think the Plachimada struggle should be situated within such a broader picture of indigenous struggle?

Tribals comprise about three to three-and-a-half lakh in the overall state population of about 3.5 crore [2012] – that is one to one-and-a-half per cent of Kerala's population. Among them, there are about forty primitive tribal communities. The tribals are not quite united still. They have been reduced to 'vote banks' of various political parties. The 1975 Kerala Scheduled Tribes (Restriction on Transfer of Lands and Restoration of Alienated Lands) Act was revoked. I don't want to go too much into the history of Kerala now. The tribals of Kerala launched their agitation after their requests were turned down time and again. The Gothra Maha Sabha was started in 2000 and a protest started in Thiruvananthapuram with the erection of huts. We had participated in that protest. The Plachimada people have joined hands in all their protests – even in the recent 'Nilpu Samaram' [Standing Protest] in front of the Secretariat of Kerala. It was the five of us – Medha Patkar, C. K. Janu, Geethanandan, V. D. Majeendran and I – who held meetings with various ministers following the Nilpu Samaram. The developmental (and exploitative) activities are invariably centred in places where the oppressed classes of Indian society live, never in areas inhabited by the economically forward sections – be it in Kashipur (Uttarakhand) or Kalingnagar (Odisha). The respective governments say that they are the protectors of the tribal people, while proceeding with activities that marginalise them and exploit their natural resources. I am not talking about Kerala alone. The scenario is the same in the north Indian states also. The arrival of mining mafias has displaced the tribals and disturbed their traditional ways of life. Tribals are victimised everywhere. On top of this, the tribals are not united owing to their lack of education and the promises made by different political parties.

Coca-Cola and Pepsi have more than fifty factories across India. Most of these are located in places where the poor people live. This logic is the same when it comes to liquor shops, isn't it? It is almost like an effort to keep these communities in a state of stupor. I look at liquor as a tool of exploitation by the elite. Liquor drains the intellectual capabilities, wealth and the general health of the oppressed communities. Also there is a trace of environmental terrorism in such actions.

I notice that a picture of Mahatma Gandhi is garlanded and hung inside the pandal. The Plachimada struggle is noted for its nonviolent campaigns. How far has Gandhian philosophy influenced the Plachimada struggle?

One of the important thoughts put forward by Gandhiji is Gram Swaraj. He argued for the independence of villages and nonviolent resistance. The Plachimada movement was a struggle for survival based on nonviolent resistance. We did not resort to any violence, although there was violence perpetrated on us by both the Government and political parties. When some of the organisations associated with our protest in the beginning tried to provoke violent actions, we kept our distance from them. We immediately hung pictures of Buddha and Mahatma Gandhi inside the pandal to ward them off! Then some of them walked up to us and asked scornfully, "Are you *sanyasis* (sages) who have wandered into the protest?" They insisted that our method was wrong!

GLOSSARY

Aadi: the fourth month (mid-July) in the traditional Tamil calendar

adivasi: literally, 'original inhabitant', a member of any of the tribal people in India descended from their primitive ancestors

Ajitha: Kunnikkal Ajitha, an Indian feminist, human rights activist and former Naxalite who took active part in the Naxalite movements in Kerala in the late 1960s; in 1993, she founded Anweshi, an organisation based in Kozhikkode which counsels women affected by domestic and sexual abuse

amma: mother

ammayi: maternal uncle's wife or father's sister

ammi: a flat grinding stone, and a symbol of marital steadfastness, on which the bride is asked to stand as part of wedding rituals

ammini: a term of affection used to address a young girl

Anganwadi: literally, 'a courtyard shelter', anganwadis are government-sponsored child-and-mother daycare centres operating all over the country

anna: an Indian currency unit, now obsolete, equal to one-sixth of a rupee

annan: elder brother

appam: a type of pancake made with fermented rice batter and coconut milk

Ariyamala: a mythological female character courted by Kathavarajan, the third son of Goddess Parvathy

Arundhati: the wife of Sage Vashistha in Hindu mythology and identified with the *Ursa Major*; a symbol of chastity and wifely devotion in Vedic literature

ayyan: Tamil for father

Ayyankali Pada: literally, Fighters of Ayyankali, a left-wing extremist group that takes its name from the legendary Malayali Dalit leader, Ayyankali (1863–1941)

Azhikode: Sukumar Azhikode, a literary critic, social thinker and orator of Kerala

chama: fox tail millet

Chandramathy: wife of the legendary King Harishchandra

Chembuthan Kulam: a clan name

Chettiar: a title used by various mercantile, agricultural and landowning castes, especially in the states of Tamil Nadu and Kerala

chitti: mother's younger sister or uncle's wife

chodiyan: snakehead murrel fish (*Channa striata*)

chungudi: a type of cotton fabric

cilima: corrupted form of 'cinema'

colony: (here) a settlement of tribals, Dalits and other economically disadvantaged people

Congress: Indian National Congress, the oldest political party in India and a chief participant in the Indian independence movement

dal: dried pulse

dei: a term used to address a man

Earth Day: a worldwide annual event, first held on 22 April 1970, to celebrate and protect the environment

endi: colloquial Tamil term to address a girl or woman of the same or younger age

Eravallar: a tribal community that is distributed in the Palakkad district of Kerala whose members can speak both Malayalam and Tamil

ettan: elder brother; also a suffix used to show respect while referring to an older man

Ganesan: a Hindu deity, remover of obstacles

Gothra Maha Sabha: a tribal organisation in Kerala formerly associated with C. K. Janu

Gounder: name of a community in Tamil Nadu

Grama Sabha: a village assembly comprising all adult members of the village

idangazhi: a traditional measuring vessel in Kerala

Indira Gandhi: India's first and only woman prime minister to date, who served two terms between 1966 and 1984

illupa: mahua tree (*Madhuca longifolia*)

Iyer: a caste of Hindu brahmin communities of Tamil origin

Jalanidhi: a rural drinking water supply and sanitation project implemented by the Kerala Government and aided by the World Bank

Janata Dal: an Indian regional political party with a mass base in the states of Karnataka and Kerala

Janu, C. K.: Chekot Karian Janu is a prominent tribal activist of Kerala who has led some notable social justice movements like the Muthanga agitation and *Nilppu Samaram* (standing in front of the Kerala Secretariat) under the banner of the Adivasi Gothra Maha Sabha for the distribution of land to landless tribals

Jayalalithaa: Jayalalithaa Jayaram (1948–2016), a politician from Tamil Nadu fondly referred to as 'Amma' by her followers; she served as chief minister of Tamil Nadu for six terms between 1991 and 2016

kali: any cereal cooked in a thick paste-like form

Kanni: the second month (mid-September to mid-October) in the traditional Malayalam calendar

kanna: an expression of affection

Karkatakam: also called Karkkidakam, the last month (mid-July to mid-August) of the traditional Malayalam calendar

Karupparayan: a male warrior deity popular in rural Tamil Nadu and parts of Kerala

kondai: Tamil for hair tied in a knot

Krishna Iyer: V. R. Krishna Iyer was a judge and minister from Kerala reputed as a crusader for social justice and the environment

kulam: clan

Kumbha: the seventh month (mid-February to mid-March) in the traditional Malayalam calendar

kummi: a dance form popular in Kerala and Tamil Nadu performed by women standing in a circle

Lohia Vedi: the Lohia Vichar Vedi is a platform for disseminating the thoughts of Ram Manohar Lohia, a socialist leader and Indian freedom fighter

Madhyamam: a Malayalam newspaper founded by the Kerala chapter of Jamaat-e-Islami Hind, a progressive Islamic organisation

Madurai Veeran: a folk protector deity popular in southern Tamil Nadu

Makara: the sixth month (mid-January to mid-February) in the traditional Malayalam calendar

Malavedar: an ethnic hill tribal community found mostly in Thiruvananthapuram and other parts of southern Kerala

Malasar: a hill tribe distributed in the Palakkad district of Kerala and the Coimbatore district of Tamil Nadu

mami: maternal uncle's wife; also used as a term of respect to address an older woman

Mammootty: an Indian film actor and producer who works primarily in Malayalam cinema

manathakkali: a variety of spinach (*Solanum nigrum*)

Mappila: the largest Muslim community in Kerala

Margazhi: a month (usually from December 14 to January 14) in the traditional Tamil calendar considered auspicious for religious services

Marxist: the Communist Party of India (Marxist), or CPI (M), largely concentrated in the states of Kerala, West Bengal and Tripura

mash: school teacher

Mathrubhumi: one of the leading newspapers in Malayalam

Medha Patkar: a social activist best known for her work related to the Narmada Bachao Andolan

MGR: Marudhur Gopalan Ramachandran, popularly known by his initials, was an actor and politician who served as the chief minister of Tamil Nadu for three terms

micha bhoomi: surplus land; also the excess land held by landlords that was confiscated and distributed among the landless labourers of Kerala in 1972

Mithunam: the eleventh month (June–July) in the traditional Malayalam calendar

Mohanlal: an actor and producer notable for his work in Malayalam cinema

Moothar: literally, 'the first one;' also, an upper caste name in Palakkad

moraimaman: a Tamil kinship term for a girl's uncle who is eligible to marry her

muram: a flat winnowing basket

muthalali: zamindar; a rich man

Muthanga incident: This refers to the police firing on 19 February 2003 on hundreds of tribals who, under the leadership of the tribal activist C. K. Janu, occupied the forestlands of the Muthanga Wildlife Sanctuary in the Wayanad district of Kerala; it resulted in the death of a tribal and a policeman

moyyu: catfish (*Clarias batrachus*)

Nandakumar: a member of the Plachimada legal committee

Neelakantan Sir: C. R. Neelakantan, a noted environmental activist and a member of Plachimada Padana Samithy

neeluri: indigo plant (*Indigofero tinctoria*)

noolankizhangu: a wild edible tuber; probably *Dioscoria tomentosa*

oorukoottam: a tribal/village council

oppari: a Tamil folk tradition that grieves death through story and song

oppittu: a traditional dish in the Kongu region of Tamil Nadu

Panchayat: literally, 'assembly of five,' the term refers to the democratically elected institution at the village level across rural India

Panna: (here) a clan name

pannadi: a respectful term for husband; it also means a master or a village headman

pappammayi: same as 'ammayi'

para: the traditional wooden vessel for measuring rice in Kerala

paral: a tropical fish called Giant danio (*Danio malabaricus*)

patta: a title deed to a piece of landed property

pattipongal: a Tamil ceremony expressing gratitude to cows

payasam: a sweet broth made of milk, sugar/jaggery and rice

Pillayar: a Hindu deity; also known as Ganesan

plachi: a medicinal herb (*Butea monosperma*)

pongal: a Tamil Hindu harvest festival; also the name of a sweetened dish of rice boiled with lentils

Porattam: a left extremist group in Kerala

Porattu: a folk theatre popular in the Palakkad district in Kerala

pottu: a forehead decoration, usually a dot

prasadam: consecrated food offered to the gods

Purattasi: the sixth month (mid-September to mid-October) in the traditional Tamil calendar

Raja Kulam: a clan name

Rajini: a popular actor working primarily in Tamil cinema

rakkiri: spinach

ranthal: hurricane lamp

Ravuthar: a Muslim community in Tamil Nadu and Kerala

sambrani: an aromatic resin

Sarah Joseph: a feminist thinker and writer from Kerala, and founder of the feminist organisation Manushi

satyagraha: a policy of passive political resistance, especially that advocated by M. K. Gandhi against British rule in India

Savithri: the chaste wife of Sathyavan who brought her dead husband back to life by obtaining a boon from Yama, the God of Death

seer varisai: gifts such as clothes, sweets, fruits and jewellery that are displayed in a row on special occasions like marriage

Sembuthan: a clan name

Sheelavathy: a chaste and virtuous woman and the wife of Sage Ugrathapas

Sivaji (Ganesan): an Indian stage and film actor who predominantly worked in Tamil cinema

Solidarity: The Solidarity Youth Movement, a wing of the Islamist organisation Jamaat-e-Islami Hind in Kerala

Sonia Gandhi: an Italian-born politician who has served as the president of the Indian National Congress party since 1998, and widow of former Indian prime minister, Rajiv Gandhi

Subrahmanya: a Hindu deity; also known by the names Murugan and Velavar

Sugathakumari: an Indian poet and environmental activist; she is the founder secretary of Prakrithi Samrakashana Samithi, an organisation for the protection of nature, and Abhaya, a home for destitute women and the mentally ill

tapatta: a drum

Thai: the tenth month (mid-January to mid-February) in the traditional Tamil calendar

thali: a tiny flat piece of gold strung on a thread that a groom ties around the bride's neck

Thottichi: a caste name

thottil: a traditional baby-rocker fashioned from a used piece of soft cloth usually tied to a rafter beam or a hook in the ceiling

thumba: Ceylon slitwort (*Leucas zeylanica*)

teppakulam: a temple tank in Tamil

uppuma: a traditional South Indian dish made with semolina

Vandana Shiva: an ecofeminist, environmental activist and anti-globalisation author, she is also the founder of Navadanya, a movement for earth democracy based on India's biodiverse food heritage

Vaidyamadam: a family of Ayurvedic practioners associated with the Ashtavaidya [Eight Physicians] tradition

Vasudevan Nair: M. T. Vasudevan Nair, popularly known by the initials M. T., is an author, screenwriter and film director from Kerala

Veerendra Kumar: the president of the Kerala state unit of Janata Dal (United); he is also the chairman and managing director of *Mathrubhumi* and an award-winning writer in Malayalam

Velavar: a Hindu deity; also known by the names, Murugan and Subrahmanya

Velur Swaminathan: Convenor of the Adivasi Samrakshana Sangham, later renamed Coca-Cola Virudha Samara Samithi (CVSS)

venga: Indian kino tree (*Pterocarpus marsupium*); it is used as a medicine in Ayurveda

vetti: corrupted form of 'veshti', a garment worn around the waist by men in southern India to cover the lower body

Vilayodi Venugopal: Chairman of the Plachimada Anti-Coca-Cola Agitation Committee

Yuvajana Vedi: the youth wing of the Communist Party of India (Marxist-Leninist) in Kerala

